THE GIRL FROM THE BRONX

A TRUE STORY OF STRUGGLE, RESILIENCY, AND COURAGE

A Memoir by Debbie Salas-Lopez

In collaboration with Llewellyn J. Cornelius

© Debbie Salas Lopez and Llewellyn J Cornelius, 2020

ISBN: 978-1-7334911-0-5
DSL Enterprises

Cover Art Produced by Kyle Mahan
Photo: Debbie Salas-Lopez on Pelham Park swing, New York.

Acknowledgments

This book is dedicated to my beloved family who helped me become the person I am today. To my daughter Kristina who attended medical school with me when I didn't have a babysitter. My love for you knows no bounds. You are the light of my life. And to my Dad, my hero and the inspiration in my life.

To Dr. Clement Alexander Price, distinguished scholar, champion of the poor and underserved, mentor, and friend. We lost you too soon but your influence and love for life lives on through us.

— Dr. Debbie Salas-Lopez

I dedicate this book both to my birth family and my cultural family who provide both tough love and hugs when I need it the most. I also dedicate this book to the fellowship of writers and aspiring writers who work to bring the stories of wonderful people like Debbie alive!

— Dr. Llewellyn Cornelius

4

Table of Contents

Foreword

Social movements typically involve visionary leaders who illuminate the path and effective organizers who execute the path. Dr. Debbie Salas Lopez combines these roles in one person and everything she has touched marries the cause of justice to the institutionalization of important social change in the field of health.

Imagine a health care system where practitioners are trained to understand, with empathy, the realities of one's culture and economic status. Dr. Lopez held that vision and was instrumental in the development of the country's first physician cultural competency training laws (New Jersey/2002) Five years later, four other states required cultural competency training within health care practitioner programs and many more have made cultural competency continuing education available for practitioners. This is a historic breakthrough in the field of health care.

Debbie's life recounts how deeply-held family and community values about justice infused her life no matter where she worked, where she lived or the personal and professional challenges she faced. Her life illustrates how the 'charismatic celebrity leader' stereotype (usually male) credited for historic social change is an incomplete and often inaccurate rendition of how social change is really accomplished.

— Maria Varela, December 18, 2018
Community Development Leader
Veteran of the U.S. Civil Rights Movement

1. Prelude: The Once and Future Leader

On the surface, my adolescence was so unremarkable that it is extraordinary I became who I am today. After all, I was just another poor, skinny Puerto Rican girl from a tough neighborhood in the South Bronx attending public school. One might take that reality for granted — a Puerto Rican from the Bronx. In the 1960s, where else did we live? Isn't this the very genesis of the phrase "Nuyorican"? As in a greater New Yorker who identifies as Puerto Rican but was, in actuality, born outside of Puerto Rico? Yet from the beginning the deck was stacked in my favor: I was a preacher's daughter who the family saw as having an "old" soul. Even when I was still a young child my father envisioned that I would grow up to become a lawyer or a doctor. Oh, and my father wasn't just any breed of preacher, my fathers was a Pentecostal preacher, which meant that I grew up in a very strict household. How strict? I'll admit we did not quite follow all six hundred and thirteen commandments in the Old Testament — but it sure felt like it. It was a cult. After all, I grew up in a Pentecostal church and I was also a "PK," a Preacher's Kid. One might argue that coined me as supernaturally moral: a Super Pentecostal! Not only did we adhere to all the rituals of other Pentecostal families, we were also community role models. My father served as a co-pastor at La Sinagoga, an anchor of the Pentecostal community in Spanish Harlem. Doing "the right thing" was therefore the fundamental of how we were raised. It also meant that we came to believe that everyone has goodness within them.

I wasn't allowed to wear pants or makeup, or even to have my eyebrows done. To reiterate, this was the 1960s. Bell bottoms, miniskirts, and halter-tops were all the rage. So, every day that I walked out of my home, I stood in stark contrast to the order of the day: Free love. Black Power. Latin Power. The 1960s.

I looked different. I wore ugly glasses and had no friends. To make matters worse, we were poor, so I had to work hard to look nice in old-fashioned, ill-fitting hand-me-downs or clothes my mother made for us on an old sewing machine when she found the time. Today they would call me a "nerd," but being a nerd was not glamorized in that way back then.

My childhood routines were well-defined and quite simple: from school to my home or the church, and then home. Period. Easy to remember, easy to follow. No games, no parties, no school activities, no sports, and certainly no stay-overs at friends' houses. In fact, we weren't allowed to bring friends to our home either. My parents felt the need to control any outside influence friends might impart on me. If you didn't go to my father's church, you simply were not allowed to become our friends. Considering my family lived in the Bronx and that La Sinagoga was located in Manhattan, this also meant that if you lived on my block, it was likely we still didn't know each other.

I was fine with this; after all, I was an old soul. I learned early on that I had to be comfortable with being seen as "different" and that it didn't matter what others thought of me as long as I was happy with myself. I learned early on that one must embrace who one is.

In the Pentecostal church, we met many people who were homeless, hungry, and out of work. Like the Good Samaritan, my father practiced the compassion he preached. My family always took in those who had nowhere else to go, had them stay in our home, helped them get back on their feet, and cared for them until they became self-sufficient. This was the natural order in our house: helping the less fortunate. The irony in this is that I never truly understood for myself that we too, were poor.

2. Early Life on The Home Front

I grew up in a hardworking, tight-knit family, steeped with love and sacrifice. We didn't have a lot of money and my mother did what she could to get us what we needed. I was the second of five siblings, so I tried to keep my brothers and sisters happy. My sister Onnelly was the eldest, followed by myself, my brothers, Mike and Alvin, and finally my sister Elvia Liz. Onnelly was the cool one. She had a beautiful voice and was always busy participating in school activities and church. She also had a bad skin condition, so she couldn't do a lot of chores. I took care of my younger siblings. I would dress myself before ironing their clothes and washing their diapers. I enjoyed helping out and being second in charge.

We first lived on Fox Avenue in the heart of the South Bronx. I remember that we were robbed one night and I hid under the bed. My father swore that in due time we would purchase our own home and we eventually did: a small house on Belmont Ave about two and a half miles north, near the Bronx Zoo. It was a tough neighborhood — and getting tougher — but Mom and Dad did what they could to fix it up and make it home. We lived on the first floor of the house, on street level. My father rented out both the upstairs apartment and the basement to help pay the mortgage. He made ends meet by selling furniture from our house, using his car to help neighbors move, and selling homemade food. He was a good and instinctual businessman, and provided us with a comfortable, working class living.

On one side of us, we had an Italian neighbor who grew grapes and would gift some to Dad. Flanked on the other side and just across the street were public housing projects. Directly across the street were several other high-rises with a playground, doctors' offices, and long dark hallways. Even though our home was small, we recognized just how much *more* we had than the families living across the street in the projects.

I would describe our home life as intimate and highly personal: all five of my brothers and sisters slept in one bedroom. It was imperative that we got along — each of my siblings was within a few feet of me at all times! That house was the joy of my heart. We enjoyed the company of family, particularly on days when our cousins came over. We had a nice yard where my father planted vegetables and roses. Our yard was very small, so we entertained ourselves by doing things like jumping off the second-floor porch into the garden below.

One day my sister cut her thigh doing just that —she was grazed by a big rusty nail and we had to take her to the hospital. When my brother Alvin got a tricycle, we were all so excited that we all jumped on it and almost broke it. It was the first time we had ever had a bike in the family. Mom yelled, cautioning: "You're going to break the bike!"

My father let us have fun, but he also made sure we did our homework and kept up with current events. He let us read the newspapers once he had finished with them—the *Daily News* and the *New York Times*, are what he read every day.

Of course, we read books from school, which my father often censored, and we read the Bible too.

Dad was also very strict about some things. We couldn't go into the front yard to play unless he or my mother were there to supervise. Though Belmont Avenue wasn't very a busy street, the neighborhood itself was dangerous, crime-ridden, and my father did not want to take that chance. The house and its little backyard were our haven. When we did go to the playground, my mother would accompany us. The playground had swings and sprinklers. I loved to go there because I could run around freely in the large open spaces and Mom sat on the bench to read. Every once in a while, it would occur to me that I couldn't wear pants, only skirts. I couldn't understand why being Pentecostal meant I couldn't wear pants or a bathing suit for that matter. Not that I'd ever needed a bathing suit growing up in that neighborhood — we never visited any pools.

Food shopping with Mom was never fun. I couldn't believe she used that S & H Green Stamp book and welfare stamps in front of other people. I watched them stare at her when she asked, "How much?" I was always embarrassed, and I would step away so people didn't think I was with her. I hoped she didn't notice.

My mother brought home whatever welfare gave her, including big chunks of cheese and bars of lard. The cheese was often so hard that one time I cut my index finger attempting to free a slice from the block. We couldn't afford to go to the hospital, so my father put coffee grounds on the cut to stop the bleeding. 'Debbie, it's what my mom did for me back in Puerto Rico whenever I cut myself,' he said.

We had a very small kitchen, but I liked it when Mom made dinner. I liked to help her set the table. When we didn't have to go to church early, we always sat down to dinner as a family. She was an excellent cook, and I especially loved her macaroni and chicken wings. I ate really fast, but also made sure that my brother Mike had enough. He was always hungry. We prayed before we ate, and we expected Dad to ask us how our day was. "Okay" was not a sufficient answer. It was his way of challenging us to communicate what was on our minds and what we were learning. He wanted to know exactly what our teachers were teaching us. "You can do anything you set your minds to, you just have to believe that you can," he would say. When dinner was finished, I helped clean up.

Every week it was the same thing: three days a week, church, for hours at a time. Like I said, we were Pentecostal and I a preacher's kid!

Stepping out of the house and onto Belmont Avenue I used to hold Onnelly's hand tightly because I was scared. Walking to the furniture store where my father worked on Tremont Avenue, south of the house, was always scary. Too many cars, too many people, so many stores. Onnelly, who was so tall and beautiful, always made me feel safe. I used to feel like a tiny duckling at a huge lake, and my mother in the role of mother duck. As I huddled along with the rest of the ducklings, I always wondered how she felt about having five of us. So many kids, so much work, not nearly enough money.

I saw in her eyes and in the wrinkles on her forehead that she was trying so hard to give us everything we wanted. But there were five of us and it was the South Bronx. Moreover it was 1967 and we were just one of many hard-working Puerto Rican families who moved to the Bronx from Puerto Rico to pursue a better life. Despite of my mother's furrowed brow, I knew by how my father doted and spoke to her that he loved her so much and would do anything for his queen. He never failed to hold her hand or open the car door for her.

We passed many pretty stores on the way to Dad's shop. I remember one day skipping along Tremont Avenue, wondering what I could buy Mom for Mother's Day. I thought she would like a flower—she really enjoyed flowers—and determined to ask my father to contribute some money towards a bouquet. As we all trotted along, I kept leaping ahead and pulling back like an old train. Each time I jumped forward, I stopped, the realization dawning on me that we didn't have much to spare. If we didn't have ten cents for a slice of pizza, how could we manage any money to buy flowers? Resolving not to be discouraged, I remembered that my schoolteachers offered us paper and crayons at school. I started to daydream about what I could make at school. A papier mâché doll or a paper heart. I bounced along even harder on the sidewalk, as my day had just picked up. Nevertheless, I told myself that when I was old enough, I would have enough money for Mom.

I enjoyed going to Stanley's Furniture store on Tremont Avenue and seeing my father dressed up and talking to customers. The owner was Jewish and loved my father. It was a means to an end, as father would then drive us to our church in Harlem. Three times a week, we took the long walk from Belmont to Tremont. It felt like forever, but I enjoyed looking into every store we passed. Window browsing. Fordham Road had nicer shops than Tremont Avenue. We always passed the pizza shop. The smell of the pizza made us all hungry, but we didn't have the money to buy slices for the family. I struggled to keep up and stay alert so that we stayed together.

Fortunately, once we walked into Stanley's I got to sit on the furniture and act like I belonged to one of the families buying it. I was only seven, but as I sat on the furniture I felt like an adult as I watched him work. He was a good salesman. He was friendly and caring. One time I overheard him tell my mother that Stan was a good person who tried to pay him "whatever he could." I was a little puzzled by this "whatever he could" because my dad was great at his job in the furniture store and I had determined that he deserved more. He should have been getting compensated for all the new clients he brought in, from within the Puerto Rican community and well beyond. I was also not sure why my parents spent so much time at the church. It was as though he had two full-time jobs, selling furniture by day, and serving as Pentecostal minister by night.

Getting in the car to go to church was an adventure. All of us piled into our beat-up station wagon and settled in for what felt like a long ride. It seemed to take forever, with so many bridges and stop lights down the rough, cobblestoned Third Avenue from Tremont, across the Harlem River, and finally into Harlem. I liked the sound of the car going over the cobblestones. I liked looking at the bright lights and thinking about what we'd do when we finally arrived at church.

Parking was always hard to come by and East Harlem was nothing short of scary. Why was going to the church so scary? Because my dad could not park on 125th street, we always had to park under the dark, elevated tracks of the Penn Central and New Haven Railroad (now Metro North). The scene was strewn with broken beer bottles and heroin syringes. Unlike the El tracks up in the Bronx, very little light escaped the train tracks, making it a haven for the homeless, drug addicts, and prostitutes. Before and after church, my father would pray over the car, to keep the protective seal of God over it as the family traversed the neighborhood. I would not have known what to do without my father there. The whole mess was entirely terrifying — the smell of piss, the accumulating garbage, and the dark shadows made church all the more a sanctuary.

The block that my father's church was on wasn't dangerous, per se. Our church was no more than a couple of blocks from the famous Harlem brownstone that served as the backdrop for the iconic 1958 "A Great Day in Harlem" — group portrait of fifty-seven eminent local jazz musicians. I must, however, qualify that this photograph was taken during better times.

The 1964 riots tore through New York City, leaving a hodgepodge of immaculate, beautiful brownstones on certain blocks and ravaged, derelict tenements on others. Still, to only talk about the way New York *looked* then sells short the vibrant culture that distinguished the city as one of the epicenters of flourishing cultural fervor during the 1960s and 1970s.

Between the late 1960s and the mid-1970s, New York City went through several transformations. Regarding the city's musical culture, the large migration of Latinx families — like ours — to northern New Jersey, New York City, Long Island, Westchester, and Connecticut led to the birth of salsa music: a synthesis of rhumba, cha-cha-cha, charanga, merengue, and African rhythms that reflected the complex infusion of Latinx heritage into the United States. This distinguished the Northeast as an epicenter for the burgeoning Latinx music industry, introducing Americans to artists such as Tito Puente, Mongo Santamaria, Celia Cruz, Ray Barretto, Johnny Pacheco, Reuben Blades, and the Fania All Stars.

At the same time as Latinx immigrants to the Northeast were being drawn into the salsa phenomenon, they were also being swept up in the blossoming cultural Nuyorican Movement,[1,2] a celebration of social action, arts, and theatre that embraced the legacy of Puerto Ricans living in the diaspora. The movement inculcated the Latinx nationalist social action organization the Young Lords, — a group similar in spirit to the Black and White Panthers — the Nuyorican Poets Café, the Puerto Rican Traveling Theatre (PRTT), and El Museo del Barrio.

However, along with this wave of social action and cultural explosion came hard economic times for Latinx living in New York City, as reflected by the mid-1970s news headline "Hispanos del Sur del Bronx, El Barrio, Brooklyn, Viven Entre la Basura" (Hispanics of the South Bronx, Spanish Harlem,

Brooklyn Live Amid Garbage).[3] The dispersion of manufacturing jobs out of the Northeast contributed to spiraling unemployment and poverty in New York City. This, along with the national gas shortages in the early 1970s and the dip in political consciousness following the Watergate break-ins, funneled into a deep recession that nearly pushed New York City into bankruptcy in 1975. At the time, it was believed that the bankruptcy of New York City would have affected hundreds of banks across the U.S. These factors set the stage for our family's exodus from Belmont Avenue to Elizabeth, New Jersey — just outside New York City — in search of a better life.

I digress.

Back to my father's church in Harlem. 1967. Every time I arrived at church I could not wait to dart inside and up the stairs into the main sanctuary. It gave me pride to walk in with my family. Even though my mom couldn't afford to buy us new clothes, I never felt ashamed or embarrassed to wear the garments she made for us. Most people in the church were not altogether dissimilar to us in that way. I kind of liked it. My gray jumper had a crooked hem, and I was a bit shy when I wore it, but I had no choice. New clothes were reserved for Easter and Christmas. I couldn't wait till Mom bought us those white patent leather shoes and cute little frocks at Hunts Point Market for Easter. She said she'd buy us coats, like the crushed red velvet one I had seen the last time we were there. I thought to myself "I'd look pretty in that one." Until then, I walked down the aisle proudly donning whatever I was wearing.

Church was always full. As soon as we walked in, we kneeled down at our seats and prepared for the service. The men sat on one side of the church and the women on the other. People stood up on the stage and sang, prayed, and gave testimony. I always sat with Mom. She kept an eye on us and didn't let us make any noise, chew gum, or talk to each other. The service was always long and ended with a lengthy sermon about hell and heaven.

The music was playing, the people were happy; it was so different from the surrounding streets. La Sinagoga was a converted theater and we children had the upstairs to play as my parents and church members prepared food for the congregation downstairs. My favorite game was hide and seek because the church was so large and had great places to hide. Though I was naturally the best at it, I always thought it unfair that my siblings maintained the advantage by hiding in the creepy, cavernous corners of the church no one else dared to go. The food was just wonderful, especially the chicken and rice, and everyone liked talking to Mom and Dad.

My father was a great preacher and I adored him. It wasn't all talk of heaven and hell but rather, he read verses from the bible and tried to explain them, to contextualize them. When he was at the pulpit in the big, theater-like church, I felt very proud. He was well-dressed in his black suit, a nicely ironed white shirt and a tie. He never wore anything fancy but took care to always look polished and well kept.

When the church service was over, Dad always came to get us. I liked standing beside him and I took pride in that he included us when he talked to people. It made me feel important. He took his time shaking people's hands and asking them how they were. He didn't like us to interrupt him when he was talking to a member of the church, and we had to wait by the side for him to finish. He never wanted us to rush him to go home. It seemed like we were always the last to leave. I sometimes overheard him talking to people. He always imparted his thoughts in a way that was both kind and gentle. I think that was the reason people lined up to say hello and to get his advice. When he had the time, he took appointments in a small office in the back of the church. People lined up to tell him about their problems. I will never forget, he was like a priest in that way.

- - -

Lessons Learned

By the time we left the Bronx to move to New Jersey, my family, my church, and my community had already instilled in me the key values that would shape my later life as a leader. These values were:

- To live life with integrity and ethics
- To believe in the goodness of humankind
- To be humble and give credit where credit is due
- To learn to love new ideas
- To have the courage to face adversity head-on
- To live in wonder and to be curious
- To reject pessimism in favor of optimism
- To be comfortable with who you are
- To be patient with yourself and with others

- To remember that a well-balanced life is as important as hard work
- To care for and about people, genuinely
- To pay it forward; to live in the service of others

Some of these principles were already part of my life then, even in little ways. I was always curious about the world; I was given responsibilities to care for others in my family; I was taught to be humble and to find joy in little things. Other principles such as values related to work and balancing work and family life would come later.

Looking back on this, I challenge each of us to reflect and identify the principles that shaped our habits, world views, and the way we deal with each other. Even today, these principles guide me toward the person I strive to become.

Notes:

[1] Nuyorican is a term that represents Puerto Ricans who were not born in Puerto Rico, but in the New York Metro Area.

[2] Farrington, D. (2013). Photographing Puerto Rican New York, With A 'Sympathetic Eye.' Retrieved from: http://www.npr.org/sections/codeswitch/2013/10/26/231704827/photographing-puerto-rican-new-york-with-a-sympathetic-eye

[3] Farrington, (2013). Ibid.

3. The Move to "Jersey"

In 1969 our family moved from one blossoming community, the South Bronx, to another, Port Elizabeth, New Jersey, in the "Garden State." When we moved to Port Elizabeth, we were one of only a few Latinx families in a community whose closest real exposure to Latinx culture at the time would have been on TV: Rita Moreno starring in West Side Story, Jose Feliciano singing "Light My Fire," *Tony Orlando and Dawn*, or Freddie Prinze in *Chico and the Man*.

Our family, like those that followed, was part of the creation of a "new" Garden State, a multiethnic garden of immigrant cultures that eventually would play a role in the creation of statewide programs that benefited Latinx communities and other residents of color. New Jersey, especially northern New Jersey, is the second most densely populated state in the U.S., with 1,195 persons per square mile.[1] Union County, where the city of Elizabeth is located, is the third most densely populated county of the state of New Jersey with 5,173 per square mile.[2] In 1980 Latinx comprised 6.7 percent of all the residents in New Jersey[3]. By 2015 the Latinx community comprised 19 percent of New Jersey.[4]

When we moved into Elizabeth, the city was primarily a community of immigrants from Italy, Germany, and Poland. By 2017, Latinx comprised about 60 percent of the city with more than 50 languages represented in Elizabeth.[5] The Latinx immigrants who settled in there were persons who were pushed out of Cuba during the Castro Revolution, refugee and asylum seekers from civil wars and ethnic cleansings that were taking place in Central and Latin America, and Puerto Ricans like us who fled New York City. Each group infused northern New Jersey with political, cultural, and economic capital that would later transform its power base.

In spite of all this Latinx influx into Elizabeth, looking for an authentic taste of home in Elizabeth in the 1970s was a scavenger hunt. After all, there didn't exist the same access to the *bodegas* and *supermercados* that had existed in the Bronx—that required a road trip back into the city. Like many families who moved out of New York in the 1970s, we moved to New Jersey for a chance at a better life, better schools, and a small taste of the kind of laid-back life my ancestors had enjoyed as part of Puerto Rican cultural identity.

In reflecting on his adjustment in moving from Puerto Rico to New Jersey, Miguel "Mike" E. Rodrigues, former president of the Essex County Hispanic American Chamber of Commerce, stated:

> I have been out of my land for 50 years. I am already adapted here and I cannot now say that I am going to Puerto Rico – but my Puerto Rico is always my Puerto Rico. If I had to return to Puerto Rico for "x" reason, then, I would do it with much love and I would say goodbye to this. But my children are here, my grandchildren are here, and my great-granddaughter is here. I have three generations here and then I go to Puerto Rico and I'm going to make a Puerto Rican that I want in my

land, that I love my people, but I am going to make it a stranger. And based on that, it is the thing that one had to think about, because many go and many move.... Again in Puerto Rico, and then they have to start over. I cannot think that the people I left for the '50s, I'm going to...many have passed and they forget me. Others are gone, they are not in the same town, the high school youth that we, that where I graduated, I do not know, [if] I return, I am a stranger. Here everyone knows Don Mike Rodriquez (laughs) in this city.[6]

(Translated from Spanish to English.)

So, it was this "sleepy" community that we moved into, and although my personal life through medical school was very much shaped by family, school, and church, we moved to a community that played a major role in shaping who I was to become, both as a health practitioner and as a civic leader.

But in 1969, my adolescent mind was somewhere else altogether...

After moving to New Jersey, I was plagued with questions. No twelve-year-old should have to leave her school, church, and her home. "Daddy," I would ask, "Why are we here? Why didn't you show us where we were moving? Why New Jersey?" It was in this way that I would direct my questions to my father; decisive and forthcoming. I, like my father, believed in the power of being direct. My spirit is akin to the coffee *Bustelo* that Gregorio Bustelo started selling in Spanish Harlem in 1931: *Café Bustelo - The Flavor That Doesn't Hold Back.*

I knew Dad wanted to move because he wanted to be the head pastor in his own church, but I didn't understand how he could just pick up and go, so abruptly, so decisively. For just as we moved to Jersey, I too was beginning to change. Note the contradiction: I was becoming more like my father, but like many teenagers I was also questioning him, in my own way. I loved La Singoga in Harlem and I knew how much it meant for me to have that ritual, shared with those friends. What I did not see or understand was the big picture of what was going on in the world around me. That, my father saw.

We never had a chance to say goodbye to Belmont Avenue — and Bond Street in Port Elizabeth was very different. It was noisy because of the New Jersey Transit train tracks beside the house. It was a small four-bedroom family house and we lived on the second floor. As always, the five of us shared a bedroom until my father placed a heater on the porch and installed bunk beds for the boys. In this transition, I made sure that my brothers and sisters were all okay. They would struggle. So I told myself that if I made sure their clothes were okay, that they ate well, completed their homework, and were prepared for school, that we would be alright.

We had a new school to attend, new friends to make, a new church to christen. Moving to Elizabeth meant a step-up in terms of the expectations of us as Preacher's Kids. When we lived in the Bronx we were second-tier — Dad was only a co-pastor at La Sinagoga. Now that Dad was the pastor of his own church in Jersey, we were officially the Preacher's Kids and that came with a host of responsibilities. It also meant that we would need to undertake additional chores because

Dad and Mom had more to do in the church than ever before. I felt like I had to protect them, to step up. After all, we were outsiders there. I could sense then that it would bring a new struggle.

Reflecting on this time in our lives, I recognize that my father had addressed a crossroad in his life: either become the leader of his own church or stay in the shadow of the pastor of La Sinagoga. It was a formative decision for him to make. It would have been easy for him to stay in Harlem, gradually rise through the ranks there, I sense that he wanted to start something new, something he could call his own, something he could count on as part of his legacy. I realize now that my dad had nephews and nieces living in Port Elizabeth, and that's how the story came to be. He was ministering to them and eventually he decided that he was needed there.

Driving from New York City to northern New Jersey along the New Jersey Turnpike was always a trip. The smelly refineries on the turnpike before Exit 13 and the Elizabeth/Newark Airport Exit weren't very welcoming. We also traveled routes 21 and 22 often. That's where all the signs for the University of Medicine and Dentistry were, and I took note. Let's face it, when you grew up surrounding by cement, no greenery, in a violent neighborhood, and lacking a sense of community, a move to a suburb like Port Elizabeth is considered progress. We moved into what was then one of many European immigrant suburban industrial communities just outside Manhattan. Still today, New Jersey is home to one of the largest mass transit systems in the world, the New Jersey Transit, with 924,149 riders per day.[7] At the time we moved, some 404,734 per day passed through our area on the New Jersey Turnpike/I-95 into New York City via the George Washington Bridge, Lincoln Tunnel, or Holland Tunnel.[8] Elizabeth is one of the cities along I-95, one of the main arteries of industrial America that runs from New England to Florida. It is also the part of the state that is known more for the smell of its factories and oil refineries than any natural foliage or municipal gardens.

It is also part of the state that gained notoriety as the location of the famous duel between Alexander Hamilton and Aaron Burr in 1804 (in Weehawken, New Jersey, near what is now the entrance to the Lincoln Tunnel). It is the same part of the state where, just down the Hudson River from Weehawken, stands Liberty Island and the Statue of Liberty, herself. This is the setting for the iconic 1976 bicentennial celebration in New York Harbor and, just a year later, the setting for protestors who occupied the statue and draped the Puerto Rican flag across its crown in protest to the incarceration of Puerto Rican nationalists.[9]

Notwithstanding our move outside of the City, we remained in an area of the U.S. that boasted a strong Latinx presence, with communities centered around cultural and social action.

True to the passion and spirit of the times, in addition to being the pastor of the new church and a political social activist, my father was a community-oriented unlicensed social worker — what some would consider preaching the "social gospel" today. The term describes someone who not only saw their faith as an act of conversion to Christ, but also a platform for social service to the poor and downtrodden in society. As a community social worker, Dad helped people find homes, jobs, and transportation. His love of stewardship was genuine. It was gratifying for the family to know that Mom and Dad fostered community in this way. I didn't mind when we had to offer our bedroom so people with no place to go could stay with us. Doing something about homelessness became part of our daily lives. We became more selfless than ever. We cooked large meals in case someone in need stopped by unannounced. Dad helped them spiritually and economically. He seemed more satisfied giving of himself than receiving from others. I respected it and came to understand that this was what he was meant to do in his lifetime.

It did, however, mean that we never went on vacations or out to dinner in a restaurant. We never went to the Jersey Shore or to any of the Metro Area amusement parks or beaches. The closest thing to true family time was an annual summer trip to Lake Hopatcong, about forty miles northwest, off Interstate 80. We loved going there. Grilling by the lake, swimming, and playing with my siblings freely. It was our escape. Of course, there was always the feeling of being outsiders — we didn't wear bathing suits but rather swam in skirts with shorts underneath. Even though I was self-conscious, after a while it didn't matter that I looked strange. I learned not to let what others thought get in the way of our fun.

Unlike when I lived in the Bronx, I had friends from school, wasn't allowed to bring them over to eat or play with us. We siblings played with each other while our parents were out ministering to the sick and needy. Onnelly was always fighting with our parents; she became very resentful about our way of life and the implications of being a Preacher's Kid. I took over the role of family caretaker — checking that my siblings completed their chores and homework. Until my mother one day bought us a small TV, we had never watched television. Even then, we could only watch it when they weren't home, a rule that my mother reinforced by putting her hand atop the television to confirm that it was not hot from use. She punished us by taking it away.

Sometimes we had to go to someone's house for a prayer service. The toughest part was getting all the kids ready, hauling everyone into the car, and then settling in to a small apartment, standing or kneeling for a few hours spent in prayer.

I often wished I was back on Belmont Avenue. I felt as though it was a home that had been taken away from me. Things were always better in the Bronx. I wanted to be running in the backyard with my hair in the wind or riding my brother's bicycle. Those were the good days. My father hadn't been the head minister which meant we didn't have to make as many home visits. I wanted to be mischievous again. To climb over the garage in our backyard so we could go running in the building next door. I could no longer be carefree in that way. I was too old, held responsible when Mom and Dad weren't home, and I was officially the Preacher's Kid. When Dad signed me up for junior high school in Elizabeth, I knew that there would be no going back to the Bronx. My father's church was growing, with just over 100 members in the first year. He was looking to expand; we considered purchasing a church on Franklin Street, as our community was outgrowing the small storefront space on Second Street.

The transition to Elizabeth was never easy. The first day in school I knew it would be a difficult adjustment. I was skinny, homely, and didn't wear pants. I had the usual pimples young girls get but no money to get medicine or over-the-counter makeup to cover them up. The pimples would eventually scar my face—something I now wear with pride.

What I didn't expect was to be "jumped" — rather, *attacked* — by a group of girls on the second day of school. They took my little purse with 50 cents in it and pushed me into a locker. It took the janitor what felt like a lifetime to find me and let me out. I was convinced that I would die in there. I fainted from sheer panic when the door finally opened. I still have the vivid image of my father walking into the principal's office to retrieve me. Following a stern lecture to the school administration, my father, the decisive man that he was, removed me from the school that day. He in turn asked my grandmother to let Onnelly and I live with them during the week. We spent weekends in Elizabeth and weekdays in the Bronx, attending school there. I loved my grandparents, but it was not home. I felt out of place and alone most of the time.

What a sacrifice my father made. All this in the name of attending school in an environment where I felt safe and accepted by a small community of peers I had come to know. I enjoyed taking the public bus from Hughes Avenue in the Bronx to Junior High School 45. Some days, weather permitting, I walked. There was an Italian sub shop in front of the school, and my sister liked to take me there to get an Italian sandwich for 25 cents. We only went there when we had the money. The worst part was standing in front of the White Castle hamburger shop, waiting for the bus to go back to Grandma's. The smell of the cheeseburgers was enticing, but we never had the money for a small square burger. Hanging out after school with friends wasn't an option. To get home right away and avoid the tantalizing aroma of the White Castle burgers, I timed my arrival at the bus stop with precision: just one minute to spare before the bus arrived. Years later I would go back, with enough money to buy a burger. To this day, I love White Castle hamburgers.

Everyone has something to offer, even the unlikeliest of people. When I met Ramonita in La Sinagoga, a little old lady who lived alone, I did not imagine that I would remember our friendship for a lifetime to come. Who knew she would befriend a young, lonely, awkward teenager? Perhaps she felt sorry for me, but she was always very nice to me—a young, homely Pentecostal girl trying to fit into the world. One day she asked me to come over to her apartment. I've always wondered why she chose me. She needed a little help hanging up some curtains. I was curious so asked my parents if I could go. Miraculously, they agreed. It wasn't very often that they let me go to anyone's house, even people from the church. I helped her with her curtains, helped her clean her house, and did some basic chores that she couldn't do. In return, she made me nice home-cooked meals, made me feel very special, let me use her clear nail polish, and gave me a few dollars every time I went to see her. But what I remember the most about her was her gentleness, her giving spirit, how great she was at listening to me about whatever was on my mind, and her wise guidance, given that I was a vulnerable teenager who needed to feel special. And that she did; she made me feel special.

I might have been staying in the Bronx on weekdays, but none of the family rules had changed. I had to be back at my grandmother's house by three in the afternoon. My parents recognized my vulnerability; I was the perfect target for bullying. I was a skinny Pentecostal Latina who wore pink cat-eye glasses that may have been in vogue in the 1950s and 1960s but were passé by the 1970s. I had tried to pass the eye test in school by memorizing the chart. I hadn't seen the teacher flip the board, and when she asked me to read it, I read the opposite side. Naturally, that sent my classmates abuzz. From that day on, I had to sit in the front of the class where I could see the board.

I prayed the teachers would ignore me, and with the exception of Ms. Ford, my typing teacher, they did. One day she walked in my direction. She was tall and very pretty. She was also very young and one of the few African American teachers in the school. As she approached me, I braced myself to be singled out. "Debbie," she said, "your typing leaves much to be desired. You don't seem very interested in learning. I suggest you learn how to type really soon. You probably won't amount to anything and typing may be the only job you'll be able to get." I never forgot her or what she had said. I thought to myself, what kind of person says that to a young, impressionable girl? As a teacher, she must recognize what influence she had on her students. It occurred to me that perhaps she had intended to motivate me to try harder. I did just that.

Each of my siblings were bullied and each of them handled it differently. After what happened to me, my parents paid close attention to what transpired at school. Dad always claimed that schools had to provide a great education and help kids feel confident, safe, and supported. He couldn't understand why kids hurt other kids. He wanted to make sure we understood that. He wanted us to be kind to other kids. Dad preached a lot about being kind to people that aren't kind to you—about turning the other cheek. I believe my father underestimated the trauma bullying inflicted on all of us. In an effort to be a good person, he tried to give people the benefit of the doubt, but had perhaps turned a blind eye to the realities facing my siblings attending school in Jersey.

When I moved to Elizabeth at age twelve, I became a little adult, and in my case that was true in both size and in form. I made sure that when the wakeup alarm went off, I jumped out of bed at the ready. I had much to do. I got the kids ready for school, got them ready for church, I served my brothers and sisters breakfast, arranged their books in their bookbags, and make sure they had the right clothes for gym and class. The home was always cold. The bathroom didn't have heat because it was right next to an outside porch and lacked insulation. We rushed through baths, brushing our teeth, and everything between. My parents kept the heat low to keep the expenses down. I upheld the responsibilities of the household to ensure that my parents didn't stress unnecessarily.

When I graduated from the ninth grade of Junior High School, Mom and Dad signed me up for high school in Elizabeth. Battin High was big, with more than five thousand students. I liked walking there and didn't feel as afraid. High school was different, and since I started in the tenth grade with everyone else, it didn't seem as bad. I found a group of girls who were more accepting of me than in junior high school. Even though I still felt like an outsider, I had a new group of friends. They were all very smart, "nerds," like me. So being nerdy and looking different was acceptable. Smart and nerdy-looking was something I became okay with. It taught me how to be okay with who I am and how others are. To accept people as they are, and that it's not what you look like on the outside that matters. I also learned how to connect really well with people so they could overlook what I looked like and accept me for who I was on the inside.

At that time, there were only two high schools in Elizabeth: Battin, an all-girls school, and Thomas Jefferson, an all-boys school. That worked for me too since I'd never had a boyfriend or even a boy I liked.

That all changed when I turned fifteen and met my future husband Frank in my dad's church. Frank had moved to Elizabeth from Puerto Rico. He was all alone, no family or friends. My dad and mom took him in. He was very cute, very nice, and a real gentleman. He was four years older than me, and when I was fifteen he gave me my first kiss. He was the first and only boyfriend I had growing up. Dad and Mom knew we liked each other so we were never alone, always supervised, and never allowed to go on an official date. Frank worked at a lamp factory. He loved his family and went back to San Sebastian, Puerto Rico, often to see them. It was normal for the Puerto Ricans I knew to work in local factories. I didn't know anyone in the church who had gone to college. I knew I didn't want that for me.

I married Frank when I turned eighteen, and we moved into an apartment in Elizabeth. I told my high school friends and they couldn't believe it. While they were all planning their dates for the prom and the college they would go to, I was planning a wedding. Graduating high school was an enormous accomplishment for me and my parents. After all, I lived in a community where dropping out of high school was common. However, graduating from high school was only the beginning for me. Given that I was goal oriented, before I got married I negotiated with my dad that I could get married and go to a community college because it had a work-study program. Dad and Mom were not happy about it, as those choices did not fit the norm of Pentecostal women then, but they agreed because they knew that I was going to do it anyway. I graduated high school in June and married Frank on August 14th, 1975. We went to Puerto Rico for our honeymoon, where I met his family for the first time. They were very humble, kind people who lived in the Puerto Rican countryside. I signed up to go to Union County College in September of that year to get an associate degree in medical technology.

- - -

Lessons Learned

I couldn't wear pants at home, but the uniform for the program was a pantsuit. I used to leave the house with just a lab coat on most days, even in the winter, and put my pants on in the car. It is said that our first role models are at home and that the core elements of my future as a leader were present in my father. Like him, I am hardworking, family centered, spiritual, compassionate, direct, and decisive. Also like my dad, a lot of the time I am a community advocate and activist. We were a product of the 1960s and 1970s where social action, civic responsibility, and ethnic cultural values were tightly intermingled with family life. It is telling that when things got tough, my father hit the reset button and took me back to the home front, a place of safety and comfort. There is something to be said for all of us to have had that sanctuary when things get messy. I would also say that my family's disposition for humility, rather than vanity or self-interest, strongly influenced the way I responded to the praise and accolades I received later in life.

---

[1] U.S. Census Bureau, (N.D.). Resident Population Data
https://www.census.gov/2010census/data/apportionment-dens-text.php

[2] USA. Com, (N.D). New Jersey Population Density County Rankhttp://www.usa.com/rank/new-jersey-state—population-density—county-rank.htm

[3] New Jersey Office of State Planning, (1993). Population Trends and Locational Analysis
http://www.state.nj.us/state/planning/publications/100-population-analysis-010193.pdf

[4] U.S. Census Bureau, (N.D.). ACS demographic and housing estimates 2011–2015, American Community Survey 5 Year Estimates: New Jersey.
https://factfinder.census.gov/faces/tableservices/jsf/pages/productview.xhtml?pid=ACS_15_5YR_DP05&prodType=table

[5] Llorente, E., (2016). In immigrant-heavy Elizabeth, NJ, Latinos and Muslims forge civil relations despite barriers
http://www.foxnews.com/world/2016/09/21/despite-language-and-cultural-barriers-latinos-and-muslims-in-elizabeth-forge.html.

[6] Newark Public Library, (N.D.).Latino oral histories: Latino life stories. Retrieved from:
http://www.npl.org/Pages/Collections/njhric/LatinoLifeStories.html

[7] New Jersey Transit, (2017). NJ Transit Facts at a Glance.
https://www.njtransit.com/pdf/FactsAtaGlance.pdf

[8] New York City Department of Transportation, (2015) .2014 New York City Bridge Traffic Volumes.
http://www.nyc.gov/html/dot/downloads/pdf/nyc-bridge-traffic-report-2014.pdf

[9] NY Times, (1977). Groups Hold Protest in Statue of Liberty Crown.
http://www.nytimes.com/1977/02/16/archives/group-holds-protest-in-statue-of-liberty-crown.html?_r=0

4. Time for a Change

I wish I had known then that I was too young to get married, but I suppose I had always felt older than I was. I was responsible for my siblings, responsible for the housekeeping. I was both emotionally and intellectually very mature, so at the time, I didn't see it as a big deal. I just saw it as the natural evolution of a relationship with the guy I fell in love with.

Right after we got married, Frank and I rented an apartment in a house that my father had purchased. It was a small two-bedroom, and all of our furniture was purchased secondhand or put on layaway because we didn't have any money to speak of. Frank had not gone to college, nor did he have the ambition to go. Instead, like many immigrant families, he worked to send financial support to his family back in Puerto Rico. I on the other hand went to college, studied, worked, and went to church with Frank. Our lives were busy day in and day out. We went out to dinner every so often, but we were careful with our budget. I had learned to be frugal from my parents, and I kept a little book with envelopes that I filled with our weekly wages so we could pay our bills on time.

We went on occasional vacations, including a trip to Spain with a tour group. It was the only time we visited Europe. We also went often to Puerto Rico to visit Frank's family. Unlike other young Puerto Rican couples, I didn't want to have a child right away because I wanted to fulfill my dreams and ambitions. I suppose I was rebellious, too, in that unique kind of way. I didn't have a child until I was twenty-nine, eleven years after getting married.

Attending night school wasn't easy. I worked all day and went to night school at least three days a week. I didn't always feel like I was getting anywhere or like I had a crystal-clear vision of what I would do with the degree. I just enjoyed learning and I knew that education was never a waste of time. Many days I felt tired and wanted to give it up. I didn't make any friends because I wasn't around during the day and left class the minute it was over. One evening I arrived at class early to catch up on homework. A young student was there, and we started talking. She was a full-time day student who was taking one night class because her other courses were full. She told me how she was planning on quitting school because she couldn't afford it any longer. She had to go to work. I told her my story, how I had to work all day to afford school and that I had done it all my life. While I was talking, I recognized that I was convincing myself as much as I was convincing her. By encouraging her to keep going, I too was encouraging myself. She stayed in school and graduated. As did I.

When the time came for me to pick an internship for my medical technology degree, I chose the nearby Elizabeth General Hospital, which I could walk to considering we only had one car. I got a job there as a phlebotomist and a medical lab technician following graduation from Union County College. I stayed there for seven years, from 1975 until 1982. I was very grateful to Elizabeth General Hospital for offering me my first job during those formative years. They were very good to me and I met a lot of good people there, even though I never socialized with them. I left Elizabeth General Hospital in 1982 in the name of personal and professional growth and pursued a four-year college program, somewhere I could have my tuition paid so that I could continue studying. I loved to learn.

That did not turn out to be as straightforward as I'd anticipated. The 1980s were not like the 1970s.

If the 1970s was the decade of fighting discrimination and advocating for civil rights, the 1980s was the decade of the free market place. This was the Reagan Revolution, a counter to the previous civil rights revolutions of the 1950s through the 1970s. It was a backlash to decades of community empowerment, social action, and ethnic and cultural identity. A foil to the values that were central to my upbringing.

The 1980s started with the worst economic downturn since the Great Depression with inflation at 13.6 percent in 1980,[1] an unemployment rate of 9.7 percent in 1981,[2] and a decline in the approval rating of President Jimmy Carter from a high of nearly 68 percent at the beginning of his term in 1976, to a low of about 32 percent at the end of his term in 1980[3] — owed in part to his failure in freeing the Iran hostages in the last 444 days of his presidency. President Reagan glided into office with a job approval rate of about 52 percent at the beginning of his term, promising wealth, consumerism, and individual empowerment for those who put their faith in him and the marketplace instead of in the government and the local community.

The best way to convey the direct impact of the Reagan Presidency on Elizabeth is by reproducing the speech he gave at a Reagan/Bush rally on July 26, 1984:

> This is a special day for us, and already you've given us many gifts. As we flew into Newark, we saw the lovely steeples of Elizabeth. It almost seemed that they were reaching up to say, "Come over to see us." And you do make us feel that welcome.
>
> Along with Congressmen Rinaldo and Courter; and our outstanding candidate for the Senate, Mary Mochary; our Secretary of Labor, Ray Donovan; and reverend clergy—I have the—our great Governor, Tom Kean—and of meeting and being able to give my heartfelt thanks to your fine mayor, Tom Dunn, of being able to listen to one of the best bands in New Jersey, and maybe even in America, the Elizabeth High School Band—and, of course, meeting all of you.
>
> Your devotion to your city makes me understand why you say, "Elizabeth is a proud lady." You know, so often when people talk of America's heartland, they speak of the Middle West or the Great Plains, and certainly those regions are deserving of that description. But there's another heartland in America—a heartland of the streets; a kind of place that welcomes tremendous numbers of

people—Italians, Cubans, Puerto Ricans, Portuguese, blacks, Irish, Polish-Americans, and all the others here that the mayor mentioned; the kind of a place where more than 30 languages are spoken in an excellent school system, and they're proud of it. It's the kind of place that doesn't subtract from America's strength, but adds to it by bringing us new dreams, filling us with new strength, and enriching the values, traditions, and patriotism that we share. It's a place like Elizabeth, New Jersey, and you be proud of what you give America.

You know, somewhere in the history of every American family is a person or persons who became American not by birth, but by choice. I've always believed that ours is a chosen land, that it was placed here by some divine providence, placed here between the two oceans to be sought out and found by people from every corner of the Earth, people who had a special love for freedom and the courage to uproot themselves and leave their homelands and friends and to come here to create something new in all the history of mankind, a country where man is not beholden to government; government is beholden to man.

These people came with their faith and their families to work and to build. They didn't come seeking streets paved with gold. They didn't come asking for welfare or some special treatment. They came for freedom and opportunity. And they seized both with such a vengeance that no matter how often they fell down, they kept picking themselves up until they could leave a better life for their loved ones. And their examples of courage, multiplied millions of times over, created the greatest success story the world has ever known.

But four years ago we knew that dream was being stolen from us. Interest rates were rising to record thresholds of pain. Inflation had come like a thief in the night—as you've already been told here today—to rob us of our earnings, our savings, and to take the bread off our tables. And all this was done, mind you, under the guise of compassion and fairness. Well, it's true that those policies were fair in one sense; they didn't discriminate. They made everybody miserable.

But did they have the courage to rein in a government that was growing by 17 percent a year in cost? No. In fact, they said it was your fault. Do you remember when they told you that you suffered from a malaise? They said the problem wasn't government spending too much; the problem was that you weren't being taxed enough. Well, that was nonsense then, and it's nonsense today.[4]

As the speech indicates, right in my own community the Reagan administration was promoting individual self-reliance over community action.

Did the Reagan Revolution take place in my home town? Like many places around the U.S., Elizabeth saw the shift from the small-town feel of local grocery stores, the types where my family went for their everyday needs, to the growth of mega-malls that catered to the individual needs and tastes of consumers. When my family moved into Elizabeth, everyone on our block knew each other's family names, even if we did not talk much. We knew of people because of where they went to school or where they worshipped or where they were seen in town on Saturdays in the stores of the marketplace. This changed because the new "town" center became the mega-mall, filled with people from many communities who did not really *know* each other in that personal way to which we'd grown accustomed.

This shift from the small-town feel also had an effect on the business community. Because New Jersey is such a densely populated state, rather than becoming abandoned ghost towns, as happened in other places in the U.S., more ethnic-oriented stores blossomed in downtown Elizabeth, East Orange, Newark, and Jersey City as mainstream stores closed or relocated to the mega malls. We had, in essence, two places to shop: our ethnic-oriented stores in "downtown" and the "mall" experience that others around the U.S. were experiencing.

Before the 1980s, average families in my community used the cash they had in hand or "layaway" to obtain what they needed, but after President Reagan deregulated the banking industry in 1982, many Americans were given access to charge cards and unsecured loans from local savings and loan banks, thus further pushing people to the mega-malls springing up across the state. It was no surprise that by the

1980s, Paramus,[5] a twenty-minute drive to the northern end of New Jersey, became the most densely populated shopping mall zip code in the United States. This community transformation was driven by both the personal charisma of President Reagan and the booming marketplace fueled by the sales of junk bonds.

In the midst of all this free market maneuvering, it took concerted research on my part to find the right option that would cover my college tuition. I found it though a job at Exxon Research and Engineering as a medical lab technician and health assistant.

I wanted to go back to school because I wanted to earn my bachelor's degree. Exxon Research and Engineering had a program where they would pay for me to go to school. In 1985, ten years after graduating high school, and three years after technical college, I graduated from Kean University with a bachelor's degree in Biology. I was very proud, even though I only ever attended night school and never made any friends in college.

A year later, in 1986, our daughter, Kristina, was born. Now it was time to buy a house with the goal of raising Kristina with a backyard in a safe neighborhood. I also wanted to live close to my parents because I was still very much involved in the church and I continued to help out with my siblings. Thankfully, Frank was very accepting of the fact that I had a strong bond with my family. He didn't have family in the U.S., so he became close to mine. Frank was one of the first church members that my dad recruited, so Dad always felt very close to Frank and treated him like a son, and he, in turn, was very good to my parents. He loved them as his own.

Wanting to buy a house meant we had to work hard and save money. That we did. I was willing to put in the hours and I knew I had to be more focused than ever because I now had Kristina in addition to my responsibilities at home. Buying a house wasn't going to be easy. We had very little money, high hopes for a nice house, and increasingly high hopes for a safe neighborhood. I wished I knew somebody who could help me.

We looked for ads for houses and started calling the different agencies. Frank and I went out with many real estate agents, but each time they showed us houses in terrible, poverty-ridden neighborhoods. Living there would not be an option. Little did I know that there were many factors that intimately affected our search for a new home at that time. In particular, communities across the U.S. were fighting to keep social programs that were being stripped away by the Reagan administration, while discriminatory housing policies that were not friendly to Latinx and Blacks were being retained. This was all occurring during a tremendous influx of immigrants into the same overcrowded, poor and low-income communities we were trying to avoid.

The 1980s witnessed the invasion of Grenada (1985) by the U.S. and the support of the "Contras" in Nicaragua, all contributing to the migration to the U.S of disenfranchised populations from Central America and the Caribbean. The 1980s also witnessed a continued steady migration of Puerto Ricans to the U.S. mainland following rising crime, overcrowding, unemployment, and a doubling of public debt in Puerto Rico. By 1990, Puerto Ricans had become the second-largest Latinx population in the U.S. mainland, behind Mexican Americans.[6]

In addition to overcrowded neighborhoods, poor and low-income communities around the U.S. faced challenges in buying new homes because of the disproportionate lack of resources available for public education in these communities. In 1981 several low-income communities across New Jersey united in a class action law suit against the state regarding the inequitable distribution of public tax dollars from property taxes to the local communities.

All these factors placed us on the downside of the so-called 1980s economic boom, as the "trickle-down effect" of Reagan's "supply side economics" never trickled down to our pockets — that's for sure. The maverick that I am, I told myself I'd much rather stay in an apartment I could afford and that would be safe for Kristina to play in, than be forced to buy substandard housing in the "hood."
Yet I remained set on a home for Kristina to grow up in. A safe neighborhood was a must. I also needed to live within commuting distance from any of my three offices in the towns of Clinton, Linden, and Florham Park where I worked as a health technician for Exxon Research and Engineering. Plainfield, New Jersey fit that criteria. I'd look for houses in the only place I know—the newspaper.

Mom and Dad always said that buying a house was an admirable goal to have. It would serve as an investment. Looking was easy, finding one was not. Because we didn't have enough money, we couldn't afford much, but Frank was handy and we could buy a fixer-upper in a nice neighborhood. The agents we set meetings with did not seem aligned on this vision. Most of the houses we were seeing were seventy, eighty, ninety or more years old. They were dilapidated and located in notoriously crime-ridden neighborhoods. It's funny how the atmosphere in those houses was so cold. Most of them had renters who didn't care about their houses or how they lived. The neighborhoods looked dirty, as though they'd seen better days. There was an affinity with our old neighborhood in the Bronx — formerly Italian and Jewish immigrant neighborhoods that were now occupied by poor Latinx and African American families.

It was 1986 and the right time to buy a house—the height of the Reagan economic boom. The fact that we didn't have a lot of money wouldn't stop me. The problem was that the real estate agents were showing me houses I could afford in neighborhoods I didn't want. I wondered if perhaps I was being typecast as a resident who would *fit in* with the existing demographic. I would later learn that this was classic "redlining." I suspected that when I called and gave them my last name it triggered demographic associations. It was hard to believe that there weren't neighborhoods that were both diverse *and* safe. "Is it possible to get a house that needs a lot of work but is in a good, safe neighborhood?" I asked. "You can, but you have to be in on the ground floor from the time the seller calls the agency."

How would I get in on the ground floor? It turned out that most of the good deals were bought by the agents or the agencies themselves. They flipped them for a lot of money once they were all fixed up. The only way to strike this advantage was to work in one of the real estate agencies myself. I recognized very early on that any house I was shown was a house that a real estate agency or real estate agent didn't want to buy. I had to figure out how to get upstream of that phenomenon. What if I got a real estate license just to be able to sell myself my own house, get in on the listing before it hit the real estate market, and hopefully make an offer if it was in a good neighborhood? That may work.

I just had to take a test, learn to write up a contract, and hone my client skills. Seemed simple enough. In the face of housing discrimination, I decided to side step the system and become a real estate agent.

I found out where to take the courses and that they could be done at night. The week-long course was followed by a test. The school was in Garwood, New Jersey, not that far from work. I'd take the courses at night and on Saturdays until I was finished. Once I passed the test, I could put my license in any office so I could look for houses in the Multiple Listing Book (a book that was released weekly listing all the new houses on the market, known today as the Multiple Listing System) for myself. How hard could that be?

I passed the test and approached a real estate office to inquire about working to sell myself a house. The agent was kind enough to allow me to do that. In 1986, I began working at night in a real estate office and found a house — a "fixer-upper" — on Dorsey Place in Plainfield. Thankfully, it was affordable and the seller was a little old lady who took mercy on us and sold us the house "as is."

It is worth mentioning that this legwork was accomplished all while I was pregnant and still working at Exxon. In fact, I was actually showing new homes while nine months pregnant — up to the day before Kristina was born — complete in my real estate uniform and all!

Kristina was born on August 8th, 1986. What a labor process. She was eventually born by Cesarean section at 2:30 in the morning. I was so relieved that she was healthy and beautiful. Frank was the happiest I'd ever seen him. We couldn't believe it was true. What a beautiful miracle. To experience the birth of a child is the most exciting, memorable, miraculous thing on Earth. We were a family. We owned a home. Life was good.

- - -

Lessons Learned

- To be a lifelong learner
- To surround oneself with mentors and people smarter than you

Adversity can bring out the best or the worse of us. In my case, in response to the national shift away from communal values, I dug in. I did not let discrimination and economic strife stop me from supporting my family and my community. I was able to do so by asserting the role of maverick, asserting myself against a strong leader whom I loved and admired—my father—but who I needed to grow beyond if I was to become an independent woman. I knew if I could petition him to allow me to do nontraditional things, I could think outside of the box to resolve other matters. Underlying all this, though, is the issue of staying true to your core principles, regardless of the noise going on around you. It would have been easy to become greedy in the 1980s in the midst of the *I*, *me*, and *my* generation. It is a lot harder to remain compassionate.

Yet therein lies the difference in the long run: you get out of life what you put into it.

[1]Inflationdata.com, (2017). Historical Inflation Data.
https://inflationdata.com/Inflation/Inflation_Rate/HistoricalInflation.aspx

[2] Bureau of Labor Statistics, (2017). Labor Force Statistics from the Current Population Survey. (Unadj) Unemployment Rate.
https://data.bls.gov/timeseries/LNU04000000?years_option=all_years&periods_option=specific_periods&periods=Annual+Data

[3] GALLOP, (2017). Presidential Approval Ratings—Gallup Historical Statistics and Trends. Retrieved from:
http://www.gallup.com/poll/116677/presidential-approval-ratings-gallup-historical-statistics-trends.aspx

[4] The American Presidency Project, (N.D.). Remarks at a Reagan-Bush Rally in Elizabeth, New Jersey, July 26, 1984.Retrieved from:
http://www.presidency.ucsb.edu/ws/?pid=40203

[5] Lanyard, C. (2005). Paramus Shopping 07052. Retrieved from: https://paramuschamber.org/cms/wp-content/uploads/2014/03/Paramus_No1_Retail.pdf

[6] Green. D., (N.D.). Puerto Rican Americans. Retrieved from: http://www.everyculture.com/multi/Pa-Sp/Puerto-Rican-Americans.html. The National Puerto Rican Chamber of Commerce (2015.). Puerto Rico's Economy: A brief history of reforms from the 1980s to today and policy recommendations for the future. Retrieved from: http://nprchamber.org/files/3-19-15-Puerto-Rico-Economic-Report.pdf

5. The Real Estate Days

As a real estate agent working in the housing market in the 1980s, I had to wrestle with problems I did not have control over: the discriminatory housing policies that were in place and the manic-depressive housing sales market. An age-old discriminatory policy called "redlining" hampered communities in northern New Jersey that had a large population of persons of color. In the 1930s, the Home Owner's Loan Corporation (HOLC) developed and submitted to the Federal Housing Administration a series of color-coded maps for 239 cities across the U.S. Communities were rated from green/"A" and blue/"B" to yellow/"C" and red/"D." Yellow represented "declining" communities (bordering Black neighborhoods) and red represented Black and low-income communities. (See Figure 24 in the Appendix.)

These yellow and red communities were communities where persons of color were ineligible for FHA-insured mortgages. At the same time, higher thresholds were placed for persons from these communities who wished to move into the green and blue communities, thereby keeping persons of color out of white communities.[1] Case in point, the HOLC produced the following redlining map for Essex County, New Jersey, in 1940.[2] I learned later from a historian named Dr. Clement Price, who would become one of my mentors and friend, that this redlining was what led to the decline of Newark in the 1930s, setting the stage for the 1960s riots.

I liked selling houses. It gave me a lot of satisfaction to help first-time buyers find their homes. The real estate market was booming in the 1980s and people were looking to invest their money or stop paying rent and start paying for a house they could call their own. Not many people in my office wanted to show low-priced houses, but I was happy to. Most of the other agents didn't need to work or only did real estate to go look at other people's houses. I didn't care why others were doing it — I did it because I liked it and because educating first-time home buyers on how to find a great buy in a nice neighborhood, how to get a mortgage, how much money they would need, were personally rewarding to me. These were skills that I hadn't been taught but rather I had learned on my own. It was a time-consuming, step-by-step process. I often drove them by my house on Dorsey Place to show them what the possibilities were. "If you want something badly enough, you have to be willing to work for it," is what I always said.

I could tell how scared most first-time home buyers were. Quelling their fears through education was step one. Teaming up with a mortgage representative who didn't mind handholding first-time home buyers was step two. Frank D'Angelo, a mortgage representative who had helped us buy our house, was the ideal person to help others. He was patient and compassionate with first-time home buyers and he treated everyone with respect, no matter how much or how little money they had. I still use Frank whenever I need a mortgage.

I've always followed the principle: do unto others as you want done unto you. I never sold a house I wouldn't want to buy. It didn't bother me that the commission I made on first-time home buyers was small. I enjoyed working with people like me. I found that they appreciated my time and I received a lot of personal satisfaction from building those relationships. Word got out that I was a great real estate agent to work with, and I became both busy and successful in my endeavors.

My second real estate sale was a small yellow rancher, well-manicured and well-decorated. The couple were first-time home buyers and were desperate to find a house for their young family. They put in a successful bid, wrote a check for the down payment, and ordered a home inspection. I met them at the house the day of the inspection feeling very proud of myself. It was a sunny day. The interior of the house had only minor issues, but when we went downstairs to the basement, the inspector found it had major water seepage and a cracked foundation. It would cost a lot of money to fix. The anxious homeowners downplayed how much it would cost to repair, but the inspector cautioned them against underestimating the scope and costs of doing the work the house needed. I thought about the potential buyers' situation and asked myself what kind of advice I should give them. I wanted to make the sale. I needed the money. I finally said, "Buying this house will mean you will spend all of the money you've saved. Let's keep looking for a house that doesn't need major repairs and won't take every cent you have." They listened, we did, and they found a better house in much better condition. Ultimately, I also made a bigger commission.

The 1980s started and ended with a housing crash. When I entered the market, it was after a four-year downturn in which there was a 50 percent drop in housing sale volume across the U.S., from four million to two million home sales, and the average mortgage rate was 17 to 18 percent.[3] In New Jersey, it ended up being a cycle where the market crawled in 1981, skyrocketed from 1984 to 1987, and ultimately crashed in 1988.[4]

If I were asked which event most represented the tensions within the community of people of color during the 1980s, I would say the publication of Alice Walker's *The Color Purple*. What made both the book and the movie so emblematic was how it captured on a gutsy level survival and growth in the midst of abuse and repression. In 1985 everyone was talking about Nettie (a character in *The Color Purple*), and we were captivated by Margaret Avery, Rae Dawn Chong, Oprah Winfrey, Laurence Fishburne, and Danny Glover. Here was a tough story about repression and liberation during a decade that reflected the same tensions within the community of color. Here we had the dark symbolism of Mister (Danny Glover) trying to destroy Celie (Whoopi Goldberg) by hiding all the letters that her sister Nettie (Akosua Busia) kept sending to her. It pushed her into a very dark place, yet she overcame the repression and transformed herself, both by reading the letters and challenging the sexism, oppression, and abuse around her. Her transformation was best portrayed in the scene where in response to Mister's abuse at the dinner table, Celie warns Mister to correct his own errant ways. "Until you do right by me, everything you touch will crumble."[5] Who Celie was before she found the letters was not who she was after she read them. She became empowered.

Such was the case of the spiraling HIV/AIDS epidemic that was moving across the country during the 1980s. I witnessed this as a lab technician working with blood. The decade started with patients in many communities, including mine, being stigmatized, as HIV/AIDS was seen as a gay person's illness, contracted from the excesses of the "life" in all-male bathhouses in places like Greenwich Village, just half an hour up the road from Elizabeth. The decade ended with the powerful multicultural national community activism of the gay civil rights group AIDS Coalition to Unleash Power (ACT UP), compassionate celebrities such as Liz Taylor, public health advocates such as Surgeon General C. Everett Koop, the clinical community, and the U.S. Congress coming together to push the Ryan White Act through Congress in 1990. This act was to provide affordable HIV/AIDS prevention and treatment services for poor patients in urban and rural communities so they could have access to medications, community case workers, and treatment services.

During that time, I witnessed communities fight back via legal advocacy against discrimination against children in poor communities. As I mentioned earlier, in one of the most important law suits since *Brown vs the Board of Education* in 1981, the Education Law Center in New Jersey filed a complaint in Superior Court on behalf of twenty children attending public schools in the cities of Camden, East Orange, Irvington, and Jersey City. The lawsuit challenged

New Jersey's system of financing public education under the Public School Education Act of 1975 (Chapter 212). This complaint led to a series of law decisions (Abbott I, II, III, IV, and V) issued between 1985 and 1998 that addressed school funding inequities in thirty-one poor communities across the state of New Jersey. (See Figure 25 in the Appendix.)[6]

Looking back at my life as a real estate agent trying to thrive in that discriminatory housing market, it strikes me as funny how quickly word got out in an office and in the community. While most of the other agents were reticent to work with first-time buyers because they felt they were too picky and didn't have the money, I took them on. Eventually, I had enough buyers (and sellers) to make a very decent living from real estate. I worked hard after my Exxon Research and Engineering job, took buyers out on weekends, and sometimes even brought Kristina along with me for the fun of it. I had a seamstress make her a little gold jacket just like mine so she could always look as professional as I did. You get one chance to make a strong first impression.

It was time to make a decision. Should I leave my job at Exxon Research and Engineering to pursue real estate full time or should I stay put? The position at Exxon was fairly well paid and came with nice benefits and a good pension. However, real estate seemed exciting and was something I felt I was really good at. It was much riskier considering my dependence on the real estate market, how many sales I could complete, and how hard I could work. It was like owning your own business. On the other hand, it was flexible. I could schedule my appointments around my family life and I could bring Kristina when I wanted to. I needed to calculate the average sale of the homes I was selling or listing and the average time it took to close on the sale while taking into consideration the average commission I could make, minus taxes. All that is what we now call calculating the Return on Investment (ROI). I also needed to take into consideration my expenses, then and in the future. Fortunately, I'd learned to live below my means, so we didn't have a lot of credit card debt or car loans. I figured out that I needed to have at least ten listings on the market and ten sales for a total of twenty at an average of $100,000 with a 1.5 percent commission to feel comfortable that I could pay my expenses and have some savings. The reality that I needed to support myself and my family gave me a very different perspective.

The question was, could I do it in that office? I had a good relationship with all my coworkers, and I got along very well with the broker. I got into the office early, worked weekends, and left late at night after I was done with all my clients and had prepared for the following day. I was very professional and always looked the part. Being well-groomed and well-dressed, irrespective of whether I had an appointment or who I was working with on that day was important to me and something that my father always stressed. I had to work the part *and* look the part. I never walked into the office in jeans or looking casual. Buying a house is a big deal for clients, a big investment of hard-earned money, and they wanted to work with a professional. While I knew that it was very risky and that the real estate market could slow down, I wanted to take a chance. I left Exxon Research and Engineering to become a full-time real estate agent in 1987. I sold and listed many houses in Plainfield, South Plainfield, North Plainfield, and Scotch Plains, New Jersey in the late 1980s and early 1990s.

One memory from this period remains close to my heart. It was 1991. Kristina was five. We walked into the Scotch Plains bagel store on a Saturday morning to get coffee and bagels. She loved picking them out from behind the counter. The young man behind the counter handed her the bagel and she looked at me, eager to eat it as soon as we got into the car. She was hungry. At that moment an old man walked in. He looked ragged, hungry, and disheveled. The young man behind the counter yelled at him to leave immediately. Kristina held my hand tightly and waited to see what the old man would do. Then she let my hand go. She walked over to him and offered him her bagel with a smile. He looked at me and then at her. He wasn't sure if he should accept it or not. I nodded and smiled. He took the bagel and left. Kristina cried. She learned a lot that day. She hasn't changed. Until this day, she helps those less fortunate and has a place in her heart for the homeless.

By the 1990s, Latinx across the U.S. were being heavily courted by all political parties for our vote. We were seen as the "swing vote" between whites, Asians, and African Americans, between progressives and conservatives. That decade was also the first since the 1960s that Puerto Ricans were being asked to vote on whether they wished to remain as a commonwealth or become a state. This was not a trivial matter. Politically and culturally, it spoke to the heart of what it meant to be Puerto Rican. Was Puerto Rico an independent Spanish-speaking country in the Caribbean, or a U.S. colony in a postcolonial world? Would Puerto Rico gain independence from the influence of the U.S. in the Caribbean basin and engage in free trade with other nations in the Caribbean and Latin America, independent of the U.S? Would it remain an economically protected "colony" with economic support from the federal government, along with limited representation in Congress? Or would it become the 51st state, with state taxing and spending authorities at risk of losing their cultural identity? The contemporary struggle for Puerto Rico reflected the struggles other islands and territories in the Caribbean basin faced during their years of attempting to become independent of the United Kingdom, France, Spain, the Netherlands, Denmark, and other countries. This was the stuff of many intense multigenerational discussions in family rooms and social clubs across the Puerto Rican diaspora. Yes, depending on your age, political party, and even where your family came from in Puerto Rico—like Lares, the center of the struggle for independence in 1868[7]—this conversation took on entirely different meaning. In the first referendum of the 1990s (1993), President G.H.W. Bush advocated for statehood. In the second referendum (1998), President Clinton took a decidedly neutral position on the referendum (1998).[8] Neither stand resulted in a change in the commonwealth status for Puerto Rico. Puerto Rico was caught between having a larger per capita income than any other Latin American nation, yet lower than states on the mainland.[9]

\- - -

Lessons Learned

One of the important things in understanding the destiny of individuals and communities is to look for the ways in which they culturally adapt things to their local context. In the context of the 1980s, I adapted Reagan self-reliance to suit the cultural values and principles of my upbringing, in particular, educating the disenfranchised on how to become good consumers in the housing marketplace. I am a doer. It is one thing to talk about empowering others, and another to do it, and so I worked on not just helping my family (the Reagan approach), but also empowering Latinx and Blacks who were bearing the brunt of discriminatory housing policies. This remained true to the principles I listed at the end of chapter one.

---

[1] The Fair Housing Center of Greater Boston, (N.D). (1934). Federal Housing Administration Created. Retrieved from: http://www.bostonfairhousing.org/timeline/1934-FHA.html; Madrigal, A.C. (2014). "The racist policy that made your neighborhood." Retrieved from: https://www.theatlantic.com/business/archive/2014/05/the-racist-housing-policy-that-made-your-neighborhood/371439/; Hillier, A.E., (2003). "Redlining and the Homeowners' Loan Corporation." Journal of Urban History, 29, 394–420.

[2] Jackson, K.T., (1980). "Race, Ethnicity, and Real Estate Appraisal: The Home Owners Loan Corporation and the Federal Housing Administration". Journal of Urban History 6:419–452

[3] Perry M.J., (2009). "How Bad Was the 1980s Real Estate Crash?" Retrieved from https://seekingalpha.com/amp/article/117845-how-bad-was-the-1980s-real-estate-crash

[4] Bednar, J., (N.D). "Home Prices Do Fall A Look At The Collapse Of The 1980's Real Estate Bubble Through The Eyes Of The New York Times." Retrieved from: http://njrereport.com/80sbubble.htm

[5] Walker, A,, (1992). The Color Purple. London: Women's Press, 213.

[6] Education Law Center, (N.D.). "The History of Abbott v Burke." Retrieved from: http://www.edlawcenter.org/cases/abbott-v-burke/abbott-history.html

[7] Library of Congress, (N.D.). The Grito de Lares: The Rebellion of 1868. https://www.loc.gov/collections/puerto-rico-books-and-pamphlets/articles-and-essays/nineteenth-century-puerto-rico/rebellion-of-1868/

[8] Ballotpedia, (2017). "Puerto Rico Statehood, Independence, Free Association, or Current Status Referendum (2017)." https://ballotpedia.org/Puerto_Rico_Statehood,_Independence,_Free_Association,_or_Current_Status_Referendum_(2017)

[9] Rivera-Batiz, F. L., & Santiago, C. E., (1996). Island paradox: Puerto Rico in the 1990s. New York: Russell Sage Foundation.

6. Boldly Going Where I Hadn't Gone Before

In 1991 I was selling Felicia a house. After a long day of looking at houses with her two children, we sat in my new Volvo and talked about her life expectations, how much she wanted this house to raise her children in. Then she asked me The Question. "So what did you want to be when you grew up?" I hesitated for a moment and then responded from the bottom of my heart and half laughing. "I wanted to be a doctor." Felicia then asked, "So what happened? Why didn't you?" "I didn't have the money, and I didn't know how," I answered. Felicia said, "Well, you seem to be making money in real estate and I bet you can figure it out if you really want it."

Her direct questions caught me off guard. Maybe it was the way she said it, as if she were challenging me to figure it out. Maybe it was thinking about how Dad always said I was so caring and so good at science. Maybe it was because I was driven to accomplish anything I set my mind to. Should I try this too? What a silly question: I never do anything half baked. I also thought, What's the worst that can happen?

Well, that was my wake-up call. Picking up the phone to call Rutgers University in New Brunswick was the first step. I found out how to apply to take the test, signed up, and sent in my check. I only told Frank and my sister Ellie.

Walking in to take the test and seeing a lot of twenty-somethings was eye-opening. It never occurred to me that I would be the oldest student taking the test. It was 1991 and I was thirty-four and most of those in the room were in their early twenties.

Walking in to take the MCAT took courage. I paid a lot of money to take that test. It occurred to me that the young students all around me were complaining about having to take the test so early in the morning, how hard it would be, what they would do if they had to take it again, and on and on. What was I doing there? There was no question I was the oldest one in the group. I started to buy into the drama; what if I failed, would I take it again?

It dawned on me to distance myself from them. I didn't need to listen to their pessimistic views and get caught up in the what-if scenarios. I went to stand in a corner until we got called. When we did, I went in, took a seat in the front of the classroom, and left feeling very accomplished. What did I have to lose? I had a wonderful career and family. Taking the Medical College Admissions Test (MCAT) only made me feel more accomplished. Getting in was an afterthought.

Two months later I received my scores.

I wasn't entirely sure how to interpret them. I had no context. No one had told me what scores to strive for, and I didn't have an advisor to explain it to me. I had seen signs on route 21 for the University of Medicine and Dentistry of New Jersey (UMDNJ) on my way back and forth to Junior High School 45 in the Bronx, so I knew they had a medical school. I gathered all my transcripts from high school and college and took everything into the office of the New Jersey Medical School's Dean of Admissions. I showed up on a sunny afternoon and was greeted by a clerk who was obviously used to seeing people only by appointment. When I told her I didn't have one but would wait until I could speak to someone about my interest in getting into medical school, she was not happy. Eventually, she got up to let the Associate Dean, James Foster, know of my request. He came out ready to give me the obligatory, "Thanks for coming in today, we will call you back" but was met with "I'm here to apply to medical school and I have all my information with me so you can tell me what you think."

He was intrigued. He wasn't used to having someone come in who had not already applied and was only looking for advice. He sat down in his chair and asked me why I wanted to go to medical school. Somehow, I knew this was the time to tell him my whole life story. The Bronx, my upbringing, my values, my dad and mom, and what I believed in. His face and posture changed over the next hour and eventually he asked "why now". I replied, "Why not now?" He understood. When he shook my hand to say goodbye he told me he had never met anyone like me before and that he would call me.

It never occurred to me to apply to more than one school. Most pre-med students apply to multiple schools and cross their fingers and pray to get accepted to one. I, on the other hand, only applied to one school. I figured it was all a long shot anyway, but one I had to take. Perhaps it was my self-confident, nothing-to-lose attitude or my natural instinct for people that made him ask me for my personal statement. I didn't know what that meant. He explained that it was a statement where I would tell him the reasons I wanted to go to medical school. "Oh," I said, "isn't that what I just spent the last hour and a half doing?" "Yes," he said, "but now you have to write it down for me because otherwise no one will believe me on the admissions committee." "Okay," I said. "If you give me a sheet a paper, I will be more than happy to do that." I sat in the waiting room and filled out the sheet of paper. Years later, I would come to know that he presented my application to the committee in a way that got them to accept me, despite the odds.

The call came two months later. The Dean of Admissions, Dr. George Heinrich, asked to speak to me. "Debbie, I have the pleasure of welcoming you into New Jersey Medical School's Class of 1996. We also have a four-year scholarship available to you for tuition and fees should you accept our invitation." "Thank you very much," I said. "Let me think about this and discuss it with my family. I will definitely get back to you." I don't think he was expecting that answer, but I wasn't prepared to accept without thinking it through. That delayed-decision-making strategy is one of the effective strategic habits that I use to this day when I need to buy time before making a major decision.

I spoke to Frank, Ellie, and my family. They were all ecstatic and supportive. I also spoke to one of the few physicians I knew. I was not prepared for the advice I got from him. He told me not to go. He told me the profession of medicine had changed and was not as fulfilling as it used to be. He had grown disenchanted with managed care and all the regulations physicians needed to follow. For a brief moment, I gave his advice some consideration and then I made up my mind. I would go to medical school and I would make a difference. I called the Dean of Admissions that day and let him know I was accepting a seat at New Jersey Medical School Class of 1996. Twenty years later, he invited me to give the commencement address to the Class of 2016, an honor I will never forget.

I was asked if I was interested in coming a few weeks before the official start of medical school, so I could become part of the Hispanic Center of Excellence, a funded program led by Dr. Maria Soto-Green to help Latinx students during their medical school journey. I accepted and would later recognize the importance of programs and leaders like Maria in the success of underrepresented and underprivileged minority students. She is still there helping students like me get into medical school. I have no doubt that she will leave an unbelievable legacy at Rutgers University and in this country.

- - -

Lessons Learned

By this time, I was clearly centered about my own space and the people around me, so I was not inclined to let anyone force me into making a decision I was not ready to engage in. I had to gather the facts and confer with my home base before taking things on. I might have been a maverick, but I was also a strategist.

At the same time, the curiosity I had about the world as a child was still vibrant. That allowed me to take calculated risks. I used what I learned working as a real estate agent and became savvy at weighing out alternative options. I also learned how to limit my time around negative people.

7. Balancing Parenthood & Medical Practice

The first time I walked into the lecture hall at New Jersey Medical School, I felt like I was walking into a movie theatre. My first thought was, "What did I get myself into?" I sat behind Dale (not his real name) in the back of the room. I noticed how he put his legs up, his feet in open sandals. I became distracted by how dirty his feet were and how he had a pad to doodle on instead of taking notes. I looked around and felt like I didn't belong. I thought about walking out and not coming back.

The next day I sat in the front of the class. Third row, seat number 10 in the middle. I had to bring Kristina with me because I didn't have a babysitter. I felt embarrassed to even walk in with her, but I didn't care. I sat her next to me and asked her to pull out her crayons. The professor was talking about our biological material: DNA. He put up a slide with a drawing that depicted what DNA is and what it looks like. I was mesmerized. I looked over at Kristina and saw her trying to draw the DNA molecule on the slide. I hugged her and thanked her for being so quiet and so well-behaved. What I didn't know then was that Kristina would always remember that moment.

Not many students in medical school wanted to come to class. But when the test results came in, many wanted to argue about questions or answers that were vague or misleading, to convince the professors to give them credit for the question. The professors wouldn't have it, claiming that they should have come to class more often. They were right. Classroom presence gives one the opportunity to ask clarifying questions in real time. I loved going to class. I am a visual and auditory learner who likes to interact with the professors. I volunteered to represent my classmates as a class representative. Part of the responsibilities included arguing to get credit for vague questions or answers. I became really good at it. The professors knew I attended class so they couldn't use that as rationale to deny my requests. My classmates appreciated me for every question we were granted credit for, my professors saw my dedication, and I learned a lot more than I would have had I not volunteered.

Attending every class was part of what I committed to. I quickly learned that some other students had purchased a "note service" — other students take notes, make copies, and distribute to other students at a cost — so they didn't have to go to class. How silly, I thought. Why pay for medical school and then not go to class? That was not the first time I felt different. I was older, had a kid, and hadn't come right out of a four-year college program. I was labeled a "nontraditional" student. I'm not sure I liked the label, but I had to admit I was not very traditional: I was a thirty-five-year-old Puerto Rican woman whose last job was selling houses. Sitting in the cafeteria trying to figure out the culture of medical school was the first challenge I noticed the students with the backpacks, the cool-looking young men and women who dressed casually and laughed easily. I didn't own a backpack, nor did I want one. I carried my books. I dressed comfortably. I was ready to sit in class all day.

In the pathology lab in the company of the cadaver we were assigned to dissect, I made my first and lifelong best friend, Ana Natale-Pereira. We were assigned four people to each cadaver, but we were a group of three. My initial thought was that the other students had already formed their cliques and they didn't want to be at my table. That was okay with me, as I would get more time with the cadaver. Then Ana walked in, looking puzzled. She didn't know where to go. We made eye contact, I waved her towards me, and said to her, "Hey you, come to our table." That was the beginning of a friendship that still lasts today.

With that in mind, here is Ana's account of how we met:

Ana Meets Debbie

At that time, medical schools were trying to increase their minority participation. In particular, African Americans, Native Americans, and Latinx from the Caribbean basin (i.e., Puerto Rico, Cuba, Dominican Republic) but not from Latin America (where I came from). Thus, the majority of the students recruited there were either Puerto Rican or Cuban. So here I was, coming from Latin America. I have been here in the US since I was twelve years old, but I did not have a real connection to the Puerto Rican or Cuban students considering that in Latin America there is a wide variation within each country. I come from an Italian background, so I had more in common with people of Italian ancestry then I did with the Puerto Rican and Cuban immigrants. On the other hand, Debbie and I had several things in common. We were both married. We both married very young, she at eighteen and I at twenty-two. I

---

think mostly what we had in common was already being in the real world and strongly wanting to come back to school.

On the day I met Debbie, I walked into the anatomy lab, looked around, and asked myself, where am I going? Before I had a chance to think, there was Debbie saying, "You come here, I need one more." Talking with one finger ... *you* come here. There I was asking myself, "Who is she? Who the hell is she to do that? Who died and left her in charge?" I joined her group and that started our friendship. I always joke with her that from that day on she has been bossing me around. The best way to say it is that Debbie is a very direct person. She's going to tell you what she's gotta tell you. She'll tell you and that's it.

The first two years of medical school were a grind. They grind you down to the ground and then build you up. Along the way you hope to remain intact and keep your family and friends and who you are, because it really is a transformation process, unbelievable. During this grinding process, Debbie used to say all the time, don't complain— not just to me but to a group of us. People saw her as a mentor. The big mentoring person. Because that's really who she is. It's that she can see things that no one can see, and recognizing that no matter how hard this is, these are probably the best years of your life. In particular, the learning process, improving our ability to process information, and to really get a chance to work with patients, without being fully responsible for them. Debbie

> understood that then, while it took a few years for the rest of us to put it all together.

Classes officially started in August. I was ready in some ways but not in others. The long days of classroom work, then on to studying the class notes for the day, and preparing for the next day's classes eventually took its toll. I was getting home late, not seeing Kristina or Frank as much as I thought I would, and when I did get home early, I went into my small bedroom office to catch up. Many times, Kristina would come in to say hello and sit on my lap to read with me. She took to cutting out small cardboard bookmarks and coloring them for me so I could save the place I was working on in the book. It's all a blur now, but I remember using the bookmarks in class and thinking of her. I missed a lot of soccer and baseball games, something I still think about today. It was hard on my marriage, my relationships with my family, and on me. There were many days I had second thoughts about my decision. In the end, I felt that my journey to becoming a doctor was actually a calling. It was bigger than me and something I had to do. I made myself feel better by convincing myself that the time spent in school was limited and that soon I would be able to manage my time and my life better. I also decided not to spend any more time doing school activities than absolutely necessary, so I did not join any clubs or service extracurriculars. What else was new? It's not like I had ever belonged to any group. While that alienated me a little more from the rest of the students, I didn't care. I had to do what I had to do. I made some lifelong friends like Ana, Ron Laracuente, Nina Yepez, Paulette Rodriquez (who passed away in a car accident years later) , and Vanessa Mejias. We studied together, ate lunch together, and commiserated on how hard our classes were. I aced almost every class I had. I was inducted into the Alpha Omega Alpha Society as a Junior and eventually became President of the Society – an honor for top students. I became a student advocate and representative for many of my classes, so I became a known entity to the faculty and the leadership of the school. I used my negotiating experience from my real estate days to debate the validity of test questions and lectures. Who knew that would become handy in medical school?

Kristina was six when I started and ten when I graduated. I had prayed that my parents would be alive and healthy enough to attend graduation, and they were. I have two vivid memories of that wonderful spring day. One is of receiving my medical school diploma with Kristina by my side. She shook hands with the dean and the faculty like a proud daughter. I felt she too deserved the diploma, given all the classes she attended with me, the many sleepless nights of studying at my side, and all the times I missed being at home with her. The second was the smiles on my parents' faces in the audience. Dad had his hands clutched in prayer and I knew that he was thanking God for the blessing of that day. I believe he was the proudest dad there. I received many awards during the ceremony. The one I am proudest of is the one the president of the student body bestows on the student the graduating class most want to emulate. When my name was announced, I was shocked. Why me? I later learned that many had watched me and Kristina in the front of the class day after day and often wondered how I did it.

What type of individual goes to medical school with a young child in tow, after selling real estate? I hadn't known they were watching or that they cared.

- - -

Lessons Learned

As I look back on this period I ask myself, how was it that I was seen as a leader while being a student? My take on both my version and Ana's version is that I entered medical school from a different place than my contemporaries. Sixteen years earlier, I had asserted myself with my father to take a career path distinct from what society expected of me. By 1992 I was a married mom who had left two successful jobs to become a medical student. I went into medical school not because of the desire to make money—I already knew how to do that—but to make a difference in someone's life. My first mentor, my father, had already taught me how to be a decisive leader. I was already a maverick. By 1992, I was just dealing out the cards that were handed to me.

8. Breaking the Glass Ceiling

Latinx were struggling to hold our own in the bold America of the 1990s. Americans outside of the Latinx community were starting to take notice of us. We were no longer just a destination where people went for a rum-, margarita-, or tequila-drenched vacation to escape the worries of the world back in the States, or a restaurant or club where you visited for some "authentic" Latinx food or music. Latinx were now the second largest racial/ethnic group in the U.S., behind African Americans.

We were also seen as the key to persons of color becoming the majority of the U.S. population by 2050. These population projections were starting to influence every walk of life, from politics to education, business, health care, social services, and more. This occurred because, unlike previous waves of immigrants to the U.S., Latinx were able to retain our ethnic identity, such as Cuban, Puerto Rican, Costa Rican, Dominican, Mexican, Guatemalan, or Brazilian. Words like promotora, la familia, fatalismo, machismo, that were previously only used within the Latinx community became part of common American cultural discourse. The pursuant political agenda of the Latinx community has been described as the "immigrant-settlement agenda," an advocacy agenda that focused on advocating for civil rights protection and publicly funded social services, especially relating to access to education.[1]

The appointment by President G.H.W. Bush in 1990 of the first female Surgeon General, Dr. Antonia C. Novello, was a major milestone in the Latinx community.[2] This was part of America's continued support of expanding health care to meet the needs of people of color, including recruiting future doctors like me into the medical profession. This brought with it approaches that addressed the needs of multicultural residents in underserved communities in New Jersey such as Elizabeth, Jersey City, Passaic, Patterson, and Newark. Dr. Novello's work as Surgeon General focused on the health of women, children, and persons of color as well as on preventing underage substance abuse and HIV/AIDS.[3]

As a primary care physician, my initial work was with the same populations targeted by the Surgeon General. I also had to ensure that our providers were culturally competent and equipped to provide care to the fifty different ethnic groups who would come from my hometown to the medical school I enrolled in (UMDNJ). This breath of fresh air into the leadership structure of the medical profession was needed, since at the beginning of the 1990s there were still many communities that were either left abandoned by the riots (Newark, Harlem, the South Bronx, North Philly, Baltimore, Washington DC) or overlooked because of the negative effects of deregulation by the Reagan revolution.

As such, we never did get back to the same level of intense community civil rights mobilization as we had in the 1950s through the 1970s. Pictures of the downtown areas of towns like Elizabeth, Jersey City, and Newark show them looking dirty and grimy. They lacked the polish of the suburban malls people kept flocking to. Northern New Jersey downtowns became receptacles for transportation rather than cultural living spaces, reminiscent of the dark bureaucratic movie *Brazil,* where workers worked incessantly on drone-like activities. The net effect of the Reagan revolution in the 1980s was the drone life of the 1990s. In places like Elizabeth and Newark, we hung on via civic groups such as the Newark Public Library, where I eventually became a board member; Focus Community Health Center, a UMDNJ affiliate with a longstanding social service–oriented, Latinx community-based organization; and the continued efforts of the Education Law Center in Newark.

There were other events that shaped the overall environment of the 1990s too: the World Trade Center bombing in 1993;[4] the O.J. Simpson murder case in 1995; the Oklahoma City federal building bombing;[5] the African American Million Man March in 1995 in Washington DC; the African American Million Woman March in Philadelphia in October 1997; and the Monica Lewinsky scandal from 1995– through 1998. The African American marches were complementary examples of the grassroots community demonstrating the ability to organize the masses to petition for civil and human rights. The World Trade Center and the Oklahoma federal building became precursors to larger acts of terrorism on domestic soil.

I decided in my third year of medical school that I didn't love any one part of the body more than the other, and at my age, I wasn't interested in a long, drawn-out residency. The encouragement from the faculty and the chair of medicine to do something in primary care was relentless. The shortage in primary care was staggering, as the number of applicants to medical school dropped a third between 1974 and 1986.[6] In addition, the fact that there were few minority members in medical school magnified the problem for minority communities. Why wouldn't I want to give back to the school and community?

I also learned during medical school that I loved being involved in decision making and agenda setting for the medical school class meetings. I loved being at the table and being a power broker. I was interested in learning more about an administrative path and how I could make an impact on the public health of a community. I decided on a residency in internal medicine and the pursuit of a master's degree in public health and health policy. The big decision was where to do my residency. Many of my classmates couldn't wait to get out of Newark and were talking about residencies all over the country. I thought about it too — I took a few interviews at places like Harvard and Duke. In the end, I decided to stay in Newark at New Jersey Medical School. Why leave now? The school had given me the opportunity of a lifetime to serve an underserved, vulnerable community. Moreover, I didn't want to uproot my family. Kristina was ten and it was a very important time in her life.

These factors set the stage for my coming of age as a compassionate university- and community-based physician. I entered the health care field at a time when nationally we were talking about how health care had negative health outcomes on people of color, often due to biases in provider training, a lack of access to care, stigma, and discrimination. Others before me had already opened doors, which made it possible for me to sit at the table and have discussions about ensuring that we were accountable to the community around us.

It was in this realm that I got to pull together all the strands that had been incubating inside me over the previous three decades. All my personal and moral values, plus my cultural identification as the hardworking, self-empowered Debbie Salas-Lopez from the Bronx, set me up as the person who did not wait for the government or an organization to give me a sense of what was important for the community I loved. I dove into both the clinical operations and community life with the spirit of "ask for forgiveness later instead of permission right now."

By the time I entered my medical residency program, there was just too much in the community that required support and no time to do it. Like many academicians, I worked at an institution that was viewed by some as too distant from the local community — academia is naturally designed to foster that stereotypical Rodin's-Thinker-image of the contemplative, distantly preoccupied scientist. That image was not Debbie from the Bronx; anyone who knew me— family, friends, frenemies, associates—knew that I was always a person of the people, what we call *la raza*.

Yet while I was for the people, I was not Che Guevara (the revolutionary Argentinian, physician, and military strategist). Instead, I was the person who built up the beams of support while stripping away the self-assuring mythologies that institutional insiders would give themselves about being "community relevant" because they had a health fair on hospital grounds as opposed to in the heart of the poor community. I was fortunate to be one of many people at UMDNJ who were a sign of the times, empowered professionals who did not wait for the federal, state, or local government to tell us what to do but rather used their community-empowerment skills to move the needle of change the other way. We mobilized to make change on the local and the state level. Such was the energy that set the stage for my critical involvement in the development of the country's first physician cultural competency training laws, and the local community empowerment zones being developed in northern New Jersey in the 1980s and the 1990s.[7]

At that time, the medicine residency at New Jersey Medical School was not ranked at the top in the country,[8] but I knew the faculty well and I knew that it was up to me how much I learned. True to form, I rallied eleven other medical students (including some of my close friends like Ana and Ron) to stay in our program to do internal medicine or do their preliminary internship in the program. I really believed that internal medicine was a worthy residency. I used my real estate sales techniques to talk internal medicine up as a discipline. I used what I had learned from my father to tap into their sense of purpose, to inspire them to do something bigger than us, to make a difference in Newark — and ultimately to make it all seem like it was their idea.

To do this in Newark would be what legacies are made of. Imagine such a large percentage of one graduating class dedicating themselves to the poor and underserved, and in a discipline that was by all accounts in dire need of more physicians. Once a critical few decided that internal medicine in Newark would be a great thing, others joined in. The idea of staying created momentum, and more and more students wanted to join in. On match day, the faculty were astounded by how many New Jersey medical students stayed to do their internal medicine residency program at the medical school. It was unprecedented at UMDNJ.

The three years in residency are a blur, but I learned a lot. My first year as an intern was scary, but I had the support of good second- and third-year residents and I had the support of my classmates. I was on call every fourth night, which meant a full day and night in the hospital until the end of my shift the next day. I had gained the trust of the night nurses, so they were very good to me. They gave me a heads-up when a patient was not doing well and didn't bother me for things that could wait until the morning. In return, they knew I had their back. I helped them make sure the orders for the patients were correct, took care of patients with them, included them in my decision making, and made sure they were involved in the care plan of every patient. They appreciated my style of caring for patients in a multidisciplinary manner. I treated patients like I was their sister or auntie, and the staff liked that.

At the same time, I came to realize that often, the staff knew more about the patient than I did. Walking into the Intensive

Care Unit (ICU) at night was scary; people were really sick. The nurses suffered no fools. I noted their nonverbal language when I intended to do something that wasn't right. I exercised what we now call emotional intelligence and focused on what their nonverbal cues were communicating to me, and I responded based on my intuition, not my intellectual know-how. The ICU nurses taught me how to put in IV lines and how to run a code blue; the floor nurses taught me how to insert a Foley catheter (draining tubes used when people have problems urinating). Working night shifts at University Hospital was never easy. We were at the beck and call of the nurses, had to take care of anything that walked in the door of the Emergency Room with up to ten admissions, and nothing was easy. The nurses were the backbone of the hospital at night. They knew what to do, when to do it, and who to call when the going got tough.

One night in the ICU I had a patient who was struggling and I had to intubate urgently. No amount of training prepares you for the first time you have to do it on a patient. The ICU nurse saw me struggling and very gently came around by my side to guide my elbow. I was so relieved that he had picked up on my insecurity but was discreet enough to help me without making it obvious to the patient or family. The next morning, he was standing at the door of the patient's room when I presented the patient story to the senior physician in charge. He looked at me and smiled. When I was done presenting, I let the senior physician know what the ICU nurse had done to help me and that I was grateful he had been there. The ICU nurse never forgot it. Every time I had patients in the ICU, he asked to work with me. I learned a lot from him.

On nights that I was on call, I brought coffee and donuts for the units I was covering. They were appreciative. They knew I cared about the patients, but that I also cared about them. When my team was on call, the nurses seemed more relaxed. They knew that on that night, nobody was going to drop any balls. They made sure the call rooms had fresh sheets on the beds and I had blankets because the call rooms were cold. I took care of many patients with end-stage renal disease (ESRD), a condition where the kidneys can no longer operate by themselves to eliminate urine from the body. The ESRD patients I typically treated were young and poor, victims of violence, depressed, and trying to get through life. There were many days I felt defeated, tired, and wondered if all my efforts were for naught.

Then Dreamer Jones would come up to the floor.

His job was to transport patients to X-ray or to get a procedure in another part of the hospital. He would state in the loudest voice possible and with the biggest smile, "Good Morning, H Blue (the name of the hospital ward). My name is Dreamer Jones and I'm here to transport a patient with a smile." The thought of him and his smile still makes me smile too. Many times, I drove home completely exhausted. In fact, I was often so exhausted I hallucinated. I got home in time to shower and go to bed until the next day when it started all over again. To this day I use the shower as a meditative transition time between my work and home life. The days were long and the nights longer. I missed out on a lot at home, but I tried to make it up to Kristina and Frank when I could.

In contrast to my first year, by my second year I was running my medicine teams effortlessly. I supported, encouraged, and taught interns and students how to care for patients in a humanistic and compassionate way. I knew how to work with the faculty, how they liked to do their rounds of patients, what they focused on when seeing patients, and how they wanted to communicate on the care plans. I worked hard to learn about clinical medicine and focused on getting to the bottom of what had brought the patient to the hospital. I wasn't afraid to walk into any unit and approach the care team, patient, or family members, confident that I had the knowledge and skills to take care of anything that came my way. By the end of my second year, I was approached by the chair of medicine who inquired about my interest in being appointed chief medical resident, along with another resident in my class. It was a true honor to be considered, especially considering typically one only becomes a chief resident in their fourth year, not their third year. I graciously accepted.

My chief residency year was filled with administrative and clinical responsibilities. Along with my co-chief, I was responsible for teaching, coordinating, and ensuring that the medical residents were learning and advancing in their training. It was a fun year. I did the rounds of patients with the residents, worked with the faculty to ensure they were teaching the right things, and helped mediate any issues that came up between residents and faculty. My love for clinical administration had solidified.

With my graduation from residency on the horizon, I had to find a job. Finally, I told myself, I could move on from Newark and work in a different community. So when the chair of medicine approached me about staying on as a faculty member in Newark, I was surprised. I was more surprised when I found out that he was offering me a medical directorship at a struggling local community health center in downtown Newark, Focus Community Health Center.

As when I was given the offer to go to med school, I said I'd think about it. I quickly sought advice from some of the senior faculty who told me not to accept the position. Among other things, it would be difficult to do academic and scholarly work if I took a job working in an off-site clinic in the middle of Newark. I thought about it long and hard. I thought about how important it was for my family to have access to good internal medicine physicians, that most of the patients in the clinic were underserved, poor, and minorities, and that it might be a good way to give back and to continue to develop my administrative skills. After doing the usual strategic self-assessment process, I accepted the directorship of the Focus Community Health Center on one condition: I could come back into the chair of medicine's office and do something different if I didn't like it. He accepted. My good friend Ron would work alongside me. I took the risk. Mavericks take strategic risks.

I graduated my third year (my chief residency) knowing that I still had more training to do in administration and in public health. At my residency graduation party, I danced with Kristina to a song about angels. I held her tight because I knew how much I had sacrificed for the blessing of becoming a doctor. My involvement in the daily lives of others living in

Newark was changing at high speed. At about the same time I became Director of Focus Community Health Center, I was approached to become even more involved with the Hispanic Center of Excellence. It was there I met Carmen Guzman, the Center's executive assistant. She helped me navigate the many opportunities for support the Center would offer me.

Here is Carmen's version of that encounter:

Carmen Meets Debbie

It was in the late 1990s, maybe early 2000s, when I actually first met Debbie, though I knew of her through her reputation. Debbie was this hot new recruit chief medical resident being highly sought after by both Dr. Soto-Greene and the chairman of the Department of Medicine, at that time Dr. Johansson. Debbie had finished medical school, her residency training, and was now a chief resident. She was in the midst of exploring career opportunities. Given that the institution did not want her to leave, Debbie was recruited by the Hispanic Center of Excellence, where I was the new kid, working in a basement office down from the animal laboratory. I will never forget when Debbie came in to interview with Dr. Soto-Greene; the director of the Hispanic Center for Excellence. The truth is that Debbie was doing the interviewing, not the other way around, because Debbie knew she had options and so she was very empowered. Previous to this encounter, I had never laid eyes on her, but the energy with which she entered that room commanded everyone's attention. But Debbie was not at all a *Devil Wears Prada* Miranda Priestly character, not at all. Debbie commanded a certain energy, attention, and respect when she walks into a room, and even though she was just a trainee you could tell she was going to ask a lot of questions of Dr. Soto-Greene.

I would say that during the interview Debbie was treated more like she was an attending physician than a resident because of her maturity and her smarts, having graduated first in her class. She was very savvy. She wasn't an inexperienced job seeker, where most new grads are worried about are their loan incentive programs and the compensation and benefits package. Nope. Debbie was focused on the mission of the program, which made her very different from most of the recruits I'd dealt with. I will never forget that Dr. Soto-Greene was exhausted after the interview. Debbie wore her out. Now I have to say, having worked with Dr. Soto-Greene, who is a bundle of energy, it was the first time I saw her press the pause button. It was the first time I saw her pause during a discussion like that with a recruit, and needless to say, there was success. Debbie decided to sign on.

When Debbie came in to work following this interview, they didn't even have an office for her. So, true to Debbie's spirit, she thought nothing of it and immediately sat right in the next cubicle over from me, as if this was where she was meant to sit. Looking back on the incident I would say that Debbie was and still is the humblest, kindest, most generous, funny boss that I've ever had to this day. You see, there are two sides to Debbie: the power broker and the regular person. Unfortunately. people do not see her coming, because they look at this tiny little five-foot-one, Latina and make their own assumptions based solely on her physical presence. Then MAN, you better WATCH OUT when you are sitting across from Debbie on the other side of the table. You don't realize her aura until you are in a room and in her presence. By then it's too late, if you are on the wrong side. I have to say, though, that in spite of her being a power broker, Debbie treats even her adversaries with fairness. She's fearless but very fair and objective. Debbie is very consistent about being a model of leadership courage, and to have that kind of consistency is really, really hard for most leaders.

- - -

Lessons Learned

My formal years of training as a physician gave me the opportunity to implement many of the values I learned over the years: loving and caring about others who need support, giving back to the community, and choosing a career option that addresses shortages in access to primary care providers. In all these actions I sought to build and be a part of teams who worked together on issues. This is contrary to the individualistic orientation of the medical training process. I did this based on the principle that it is not "all about me," but what is important to those around me. So, when we engaged in supporting each other, it was in the spirit of the notion that a rising tide lifts all boats—that it was better to have a bunch of us succeed rather than just one person.

[1] Desapio, L., (2006). Latino Civic and Political Participation in Tienda, M. & Mitchell F. (eds), Hispanics and the Future of America. National Research Council (US) Panel on Hispanics in the United States. Washington, DC: https://www.ncbi.nlm.nih.gov/books/NBK19906/

[2] National Library of Medicine, (N.D.). Dr. Antonia Novello. https://cfmedicine.nlm.nih.gov/physicians/biography_239.html

[3] Office of the Surgeon General, (N.D.). Antonia C. Novello (1990–1993). https://www.surgeongeneral.gov/about/previous/bionovello.html

[4] CNN Library (2017). 1993 World Trade Center Bombing Fast Facts. http://www.cnn.com/2013/11/05/us/1993-world-trade-center-bombing-fast-facts/

[5] History.com, (N.D). Oklahoma City bombing: April 19, 1995. http://www.history.com/topics/oklahoma-city-bombing

[6] Association of American Medical Colleges (AAMC), (1987). Association of American Medical Colleges 1986–87 Annual Report. Retrieved from: https://www.aamc.org/download/374956/data/ar_1986-1987.pdf

[7] Hyman, W., (1998). Enterprise Communities, Black Business, and Unemployment, 53 Wash. U. J. Urb. & Contemp. L. Retrieved from: http://openscholarship.wustl.edu/law_urbanlaw/vol53/iss1/4

[8] For example, in 2004, the UMDNJ Newark Campus was not among the top 50 research oriented medical schools in the U.S. as listed by the U.S. News and World reports to 50 U.S. Medical Schools See Special report. America's best graduate schools. Schools of Medicine. The top schools: research. (2004). U.S. News & World Report, 136(12), 72.

9. Community Leadership & Policy Making

My decision to become a health administrator placed me directly in the center of community life in Newark, where many transformational forces were at play. In particular, the 1960s and 1970s Newark riots by African Americans and Latinx against police brutality, housing, and employment discrimination led to open dialogues that in turn led to shifts in political power.[1] The riots also set the stage for the development of a local Latinx community social service agency called FOCUS[2] (the predecessor to the UMDNJ Focus Community Health Center that I was now directing) as well as the community-empowerment activities of scholars such as my mentor, the late Dr. Clement Price, founder of the annual Marion Thompson Wright (MTW) Lecture Series (in 1967) and former director of the Rutgers Institute on Ethnicity, Culture, and the Modern Experience (IECME). Forces like these laid the foundation for the work I was about to do in the community as it related to directing the Focus Community Health Center, working with the Hispanic Center for Excellence, and influencing statewide health policy.

I first met Dr. Clem Price, who would later be named the Newark City Historian at the Newark Public Library Board, in 2000. It was Clem's smile and presence that caught me. He said, "Sit next to me." In reflecting on our first meeting Clem noted, "when I saw Debbie mentoring women at UMNDJ, I knew what that was all about." When we all met for lunch in 2014, before he passed away, Clem stated that he "hasn't met anyone like Debbie since she departed UMDNJ" and that he believed he would have had a closer relationship with UMDNJ if she was still there. Clem was always an optimist, irrespective of the situation. He followed his passion. He was dynamic. He had swagger. To put it in his words: "I can be highbrow or lowbrow." At the same time Clem labeled me a "firebrand" and someone who is "vigilant." It is safe to say that in many ways we were kindred spirits. In his capacity as director of IECME, Clem focused on preserving culture within the community. I was in the medical school and in Focus Community Health Center, focusing on the intersection of culture, race, and gender in the delivery of health services in the medical center. His appreciation of his family and cultural legacy, and support of family and religious values resonated with my values. He often advised me to "stay connected to the better angels of your culture" through keeping in touch with the memories of my community, which I took to heart when writing this book.

Soon after we met, Clem made me one of the first four Gus Heningburg Fellows at IECME. This fellowship program recruited potential leaders in Newark and focused on increasing their civic engagement skills. He also focused on building in us what he called "navigational instinct," which was "having tenacity, being credentialed and bringing to the table something that was not there before." During this fellowship program, Clem focused on getting us to listen to each other, to become passionate about learning the history of the community and how it affects current affairs, to learn how to talk civilly with those opposite to us, and to be okay with poking fun at ourselves. Finally, we learned to pay attention not to how people dressed or looked, but rather their capacity to get things done, when building our own teams. One of the greatest honors I had was having Clem conduct a grand rounds presentation in the hospital to a room filled with hospital administrators and faculty. The focus of his presentation was on the interconnection between the community context and the delivery of services as a hospital.

Through Clem's mentorship, I learned many pearls that stuck with me, including the importance of having compassion for humanity as a default way of dealing with people, and understanding the importance of developing natural connections with people and in so doing make it easy to reach out to others when needed. On a less serious note, I learned the term "bonehead" from him. I miss Clem dearly.

Directing Focus Community Health Center was my first administrative position in medicine. I took care of older, vulnerable patients of color in the middle of Newark. I convinced other physicians and specialists to spend time in the clinic with me. It worked. They loved it as much as I did. Real community medicine, for people who really needed it. Seeing patients who speak another language, have low literacy levels, and many social issues isn't easy. It takes time, thoughtfulness, and compassion. In my commitment to giving back to the community, I also taught the medicine residents at the hospital, did floor rounds with them, and was involved in educational matters. But my administrative task to make a small community center work was engaging. Some faculty members scratched their heads and wondered why I would do this. If I was destined for greater things, why start in a literal hole in the wall on Broad Street? My feeling was, why not do things no one else wanted to do or cared to do?

I came to the realization that if I really wanted to make a difference, I would need a seat at the table where the big decisions were being made. It occurred to me that these decisions weren't only being made at the medical school. Because we were a state-run school, decisions that affected the school and therefore the community were made at the state level. Intuitively, though, I also understood the untapped power that community gatekeepers and stakeholders had in leveraging social change that would benefit the same community. That realization was a game-changer for me. I decided to get inside and do so with credibility, so I would need a master's in public health and training in health policy. I understood that MPH programs focus on overall population health, and health policy would complement the clinical training I already had, so I went back to school. At the time, New Jersey Medical School had a joint master's program with New Jersey Institute of Technology and Rutgers University Newark campus. I enrolled the summer I graduated from my residency program and began classes in September of that year. I decided I would take one, or no more than two, night classes. After all, I already had a day job as a doctor and a night job as a mom and wife. I already felt enough guilt for all the nights away from home. It took me six years to finish. I met some really great people, like John Petillo (who in later years became the president of UMDNJ) and Linda Holmes, who taught me a lot about public health and leadership.

The 1990s turned out to be a tough decade for hospitals in New Jersey. Factors such as the elimination of rate setting for local hospitals, full reimbursement for charity care, and cutbacks in federal payments to hospitals led to a dramatic decline in hospital performance. In 1992 Governor Jon Corzine issued Executive Order 39, which led to the closure of noncompetitive hospitals across the state. Between 1995 and 2006 some eighteen hospitals were closed in New Jersey, twelve of which were in urban areas. The hospitals in these urban communities provided charity care or care to Medicaid patients, care to patients who are typically sicker when admitted to the hospital, or services to patients who heavily relied on the emergency department for their health care needs. Within the Newark metro area, the hospital closures resulted in a more than 50 percent drop in the number of hospital beds. Similarly, UMDNJ had the second highest charity care rate (23 percent) of these urban hospitals, behind Jersey City Medical Center (28 percent). The cutbacks in support services to the poor placed great pressure on UMDNJ and similar hospitals to survive.[3]

While all this was going on there were also transitions taking place in my dad's life that affected my work life. Back in 1996 he had retired as pastor of the church in Elizabeth. Both he and my mom moved back to Puerto Rico to be with our family. However, by 2000, my dad's health started to decline and so my parents moved to my house in New Jersey. I knew I could look after him and ensure that he received the medical care he needed. Somehow, like the energies that were starting to swirl outside of UMDNJ, I anticipated that a bunch of things were soon going to come to a head in both my personal and professional life.

They say truth is stranger than fiction. And in true fashion, the millennium ended with more hype than when H.G. Wells terrified America on the night of October 30th, 1938 when he broadcast over national radio about Martians invading Grover's Mill, New Jersey, in War of the Worlds, creating mass panic across the United States. Our War of the Worlds-type hype was the crisis related to the Y2K bug, an issue that goes back to the 1960s but only started to come to light in 1998. By the end of the last millennium, the internet became to the world what radio was in the 1930s, the current that runs through all of us. Thanks to the effectiveness of email and the internet, the story about the Y2K bug created a worldwide obsession about the potential crash of all computer systems.

Before microcomputers and the internet, when we had computers that took up entire office floors, computer engineers developed software that was based on the calendar year, beginning with 19 for 1961, 1981, and so on, instead of a four-digit number for the year, like 1961. This was because, like everything in the computer industry, it took a lot of space to generate information. A great movie to see to place this in perspective is the 2016 movie Hidden Figures, where Taraji Henson portrays the African American NASA scientist Katherine G. Johnson, who along with NASA scientist Dorothy Vaughan played a critical role in women of color being recognized as scientists in the 1960s at NASA. In the movie, the viewer watches their transition from being human computers based on their ability to remember complex math formulae to leading others in working the first mainframe computer at NASA, a computer that required a team of staff to program and manage. In that context, it was too expensive to write computer code that would accommodate two extra spaces for a date, and so the seeds were planted for the end-of-the-millennium panic. Like the tiny seed that becomes a large oak tree, by 1999 this issue had spun out of control, for it affected major systems including airplanes, banks, and power plants. By 1999, people were imagining flying in an airplane and the computer systems shutting down in midair and the plane plummeting down to the ground.[4] They were singing Prince's song in earnest: "Two thousand, zero, zero, parties over with, out of time, so we're gonna party like it's 1999!" It got so bad that people created bunkers, wilderness survival boot camps, and last but not least, law suits galore.[5] Like many organizations around us, both the Focus Community Health Center and the UMDNJ campus in general were caught up in creating data backup plans and alternative fiscal systems in case it all crashed for us as well.

January 1, 2000, the panic was over. Unfortunately, while the intelligence community was already alerted to the possibility of domestic terrorism, based on the events of the 1990s, we were in for a terrible shock that obscured the Y2K bug. Everything changed on the morning of September 11, 2001, when American Airlines Flight 11 struck Tower 1 of the World Trade Center in lower Manhattan at 8:46 a.m.; followed by United Airlines Flight 175 striking the South Tower of the World Trade Center at 9:03 a.m.; American Airlines Flight 77 crashing into the Pentagon at 9:37 a.m.; and hijackers crashing United Airlines flight 93 in Shanksville, PA. For the first time in U.S. history, all air traffic was brought to a grinding stop.[6,7] The financial markets on Wall Street promptly shut down on that morning and did not reopen until September 17, 2001. Nine-eleven also led to putting in place procedures at the ports that resulted in a disproportionate loss in jobs for African and Latinx working at the ports.[8] Aside from where we were as we watched the Twin Towers collapse, the second effect for those of us who lived in the New York metro area was the smell of gas, oil, dust, and humanity that drifted from the Twin Towers to New Jersey, the rest of New York City, Long Island, New York, and Connecticut. It was reported that 91,000 liters of jet fuel and 10,000,000 tons of building materials drifted across this area.[9] Yet the physical description of the events of that day does not capture the effect on the workers who died and their families and the ensuing activities to respond to the overwhelming crisis. There was also a curious ripple effect for families in the U.S. who sent money, food, and other goods to their families outside the U.S. The terrorist bombing led to a drastic curtailing of the export of these items to families outside the U.S. Like my family, many New Jersey Latinx families had relatives back in the Caribbean and Latin America who relied on these periodic packages to make ends meet. This dried up immediately after 9/11. The disaster also affected industries that developed secondary markets based on products from the U.S., such as the auto parts industry and Goodwill, which ship items from the U.S. to needy communities around the world.

Ten years later, in an interview with a local newspaper, a thirty-nine-year-old Puerto Rican mom from New Jersey, Lizbeth DeJesus, describes the impact of that day. (She still cannot discard the trousers and olive-green tunic she wore that day.) Lizbeth usually took the NJ transit train into Manhattan for work. The city was in chaos. Trains were not working, and she was worried because her brother worked in the Pentagon. As it turned out, her brother did not make it to work that day because of car trouble, but he told her to get away from the area where the attacks occurred. After Lizabeth reunited with her husband and her son in the Bronx the following day, she worried about the immediate implications of 9/11 for them. "I could not imagine a peaceful future, and with two men you start thinking about war, and what would happen if they had to go."[10] Even talking about this some sixteen years later brings back powerful emotions. For example, at UMDNJ we all remember where we were when we learned about the plane crashing into the first tower. Our first reaction was that someone had made a mistake and then we came to the horrific realization that this was an intentional attack on the United States. In the days and years that followed, we lived and worked in the very diverse community of Newark, worried about how to balance equity and access to health care given what we had just endured.

While we were going though tremendous grief and turmoil, for federal politicians, a crisis became opportunity, particularly as it related to immigration policy. One person's terrorism was another person's opportunity to curtail the migration of persons of color into the U.S. No more than sixty-five days after 9/11 (October 25, 2001), the U.S. House of Representatives passed H.R.3162 by a vote of 357 to 66. This was followed the next day by the Senate passing S.1510 by a vote of 98 to 1 and the bill being signed into law by President G.W. Bush on the same day. This bill became what is known as the USA Patriot Act, Public Law 107-56 (Uniting and Strengthening America by Providing Appropriate Tools Required to Intercept and Obstruct Terrorism Act of 2001), which allowed the president to indefinitely detain immigrants, gave law enforcement offices permission to search homes and businesses without permission, and gave the FBI authority to search telephone, email, and financial records without a court order. While the USA Patriot Act was passed in record timing, it is said that the core of this legislation was developed in reaction to the Oklahoma City Federal Building Bombing several years earlier.[11]

The passage of the act both changed how the U.S. would address terrorists and also spawned hatred and fear against persons of the Islamic faith and persons that people thought "looked" Muslim, which included Latinx. It also changed Americans' stance toward immigration. We became less of a country that embraced immigrants, even immigrants with marketable skills, and more a country that strove to use the Patriot Act to detain or deport persons without giving them access to legal counsel. As the Twin Towers were right across the Hudson River from New Jersey, this fear of "terrorists" enveloped the New York metro area and affected the daily lives of those in the area. In reaction to the attack, people engaged in colorism prejudice, lumping brown-skinned Latinx in with immigrants from the Middle East and treating us all with disgust. Shortly after 9/11, the New Jersey legislature passed a harsh rule for obtaining licenses that made it challenging for immigrants to drive to work. This was supplemented by Latinx day workers being harassed, particularly in Freehold, Bergenfield, Summit, and Morristown.[12]

This wave of anti-immigrant sentiment affected not only the Latinx community in the Northeast, but also others across the U.S. One example is the anti-immigrant sentiment against Mexicans in 2005 by the "Minutemen" militia, a group of 1,200 armed Americans who patrolled a twenty-three-mile segment of the Arizona-Mexico border to hinder undocumented immigrants from entering the U.S. from Mexico.[13] This led to similar tactics in other border states.

In the same year, Hurricane Katrina, a category 5 hurricane, struck New Orleans and surrounding areas on August 30, resulting in the mass evacuation of New Orleans along with hundreds of thousands of people in Louisiana, Mississippi, and Alabama. It is estimated to have caused more than $100 billion in damages, disproportionately affecting poor African Americans.[14] However, it was the delayed reaction in responding to this incident both by President G.W. Bush and the Federal Emergency Management Agency (FEMA) that caused the greatest consternation around the world.[15] The response had a direct impact on G.W. Bush's 2008 presidential campaign.[16]

For us at UMDNJ and the Focus Community Health Center, these waves of anti-immigrant sentiment brought us front and center back to the need to develop a culturally competent labor force to help providers overcome provider bias in the delivery of health care services. Nationally, the commitment to the needs of persons of color continued via the release in 2001 of the Institute of Medicine's (IOM) Unequal Treatment: Confronting Racial and Ethnic Disparities in Health Care, which challenged providers and institutions across the U.S. to reduce racial and ethnic disparities in the delivery of quality health services.

By the middle of the decade there was also a national pushback within the grassroots community, following the attempt to pass H.R.4437 (Border Protection, Anti-terrorism and Illegal Immigration Control Act) in 2005. This bill would have made criminal felonies of immigration violations. It was expected that this law would have resulted in the increased enforcement of punitive immigration laws, reductions in access to social services and educational support for undocumented immigrants, and penalties being levied against providers of services to undocumented immigrants. Between 2006 and 2008, several million had mobilized in protest against anti-immigrant legislative activity, contributing to voters having an impact on the 2008 Obama election in Latinx swing states such as Nevada, New Mexico, Colorado, and Florida.[17]

Somehow, all of the concerns regarding terrorism and immigrants did not negatively affect the ongoing national real estate boom. However, the problems of segregation and economics I mentioned earlier continued to haunt Latinx and Blacks during the same so-called real estate boom. Like many communities across the U.S., New Jersey was caught in the midst of the boom, along with a shift in community patterns. Given that the redlining issue was not quite resolved in New Jersey, Latinx and Blacks were restricted from moving out into better communities and thus when the boom came, they were left without the equity in their properties needed to qualify for conventional loans. This, along with their work profiles, resulted in their only qualifying for readily available suboptimal mortgages.[18] As a result, when the housing market crashed in 2008, they were left holding the bag, so to speak. They were blamed for poor decisions that were actually made by the banking and investment industry. Between 2001 and 2005, there was a 129 percent increase in mortgages for Latinx. This was followed by a subsequent 76 percent drop in the number of mortgages for Latinx across the country between 2012 and 2015.[19]

In response to the 2008 crash, some northern New Jersey communities leaned on foreign investors, while others brokered interpersonal relationships to fill in the gaps. For example, on one end, the excess condo market in Jersey City survived as a result of foreign investment that put a premium on building up communities closer to Manhattan, like Hoboken, West New York, and Weehawken, particularly places that gave "air rights" over the view of Manhattan from the Hudson River, contributing to the re-gentrification of communities that had been abandoned decades earlier. On the other hand, the housing market in Newark survived as a result of Mayor Cory Booker bringing outsiders into Newark through expanding office space, building a new light rail line, and building 2,500 low-income housing units, all through capital provided by Goldman Sachs and private foundations.

However, Mayor Booker was criticized by community leaders such as Dr. Clement Price for his lack of inclusion of the community in his development plans. In reflecting on the legacy of Corey Booker, Dr. Price noted that "Not only was he an outsider, but he brought in outsiders."[20] Thus, even though there were attempts to benefit the Latinx and Black community, unlike the 1960s and '70s, it was not community driven and it was fragmented. This all led to the bittersweet ending of my time at UMNDJ and my transition to a new position in Allentown, PA. This period ended with another Puerto Rican from the Bronx, Justice Sonia Sotomayor, being sworn in as the first Latina Supreme Court Justice in 2009.

In 2002, my dad became ill. We were leaving for an Easter weekend to the New Jersey shore and I recall him asking me not to leave him. I'll never forget how he held on to my arm. He told me that he didn't feel well but could not say why. By this time, Dad had developed some mild Alzheimer's dementia and I thought he was just afraid to be alone with Mom. I assured him that he would be okay, and we left. I had noticed how fragile he had been lately and that his short-term memory had been getting worse. Every weekend I took Dad to the bank to get money and I gave it to him to count. He loved to count the money and could do it well. I also took him to the local Dunkin Donuts and let him get out of the car and go into the shop alone with my order. I knew he would forget so I always parked my car where they could see me and would know what to serve him, no matter what he ordered. I got the call that evening that Dad had chest pains and was being taken to the hospital. I came back right away and transferred him to University Hospital where I knew he would get the best possible care from people I knew. He was admitted to the ICU where we were told he had acute renal failure and a large blockage in one of his main arteries. They took great care of him, but I knew that these were his final days. He would become so delirious at night that he would get out of bed, pull out all of his IV lines, and look under the bed to try to find his shoes. He just wanted to go home. So that's what we did. We took him home. His last thirty days of life were full of joy, song, and the people he loved and who loved him back. His church friends came every night to play the guitar and sing songs to him. My best friend, Ana, was my salvation. She took over his care, worked with the hospice nurses, and drove to my house almost every day so that I could be his daughter and not worry about his care. Till this day, I believe that our friendship was fate. Years later I would do the same for her father who died at a very young age from lung cancer. The night my father died, I asked my siblings to go into the dining room where we had assembled a makeshift bedroom for him to say goodbye. It was the last time he would open his eyes, smile, and ask us to take care of Mom.

Work became my distraction from the loss after my father's death. I began to work with Linda Homes, my previous professor who was then at the State Department of Health, on issues related to disparities and cultural competency. It was work that the Office in the State took on with the blessing of the governor and as a result became relatively high profile. I worked with her to develop state reports on disparities, equity, and cultural competency. This work was near to my heart and that I felt much more passionate about than traditional research and academic work. I helped write state reports that were later published on the subject and I became very involved with other local community-based organizations that served the vulnerable and poor. As a result, I started programs within New Jersey Medical School like the Multicultural Center for Culture and Language, training programs for students on cultural competency and language-appropriate services, and ultimately a training manual that would later be published by the state and used by the New Jersey Hospital Association as a training tool for hospitals and which still exists today.

My level of involvement in both academic and community issues that affected the delivery of health services to people of color got me noticed by the State Board of Medical Examiners, and I was appointed by Governor Richard Codey to serve on this board at this critical time. The work of cultural competency was being presented as a requirement for licensure to practice medicine in the state. An expert and champion were needed if it was to move forward and succeed. I became involved with experts on cultural competency such as Dr. Robert Like, who had done work in this area for many years and who became my mentor. The legislative champion was a local senator from Mercer County, NJ. After being passed into law, it was approved by the State Board of Medical Examiners that all physicians needed six continuing medical education credits in cultural awareness and language services to get their license to practice medicine in the State of New Jersey.

I'll never forget the day in Trenton when I sat back in my chair recalling the days when I had to be a child interpreter for my mom, and I said to myself, a small victory for those who are vulnerable: Now we require all physicians to learn about the impact of culture and language before they can be licensed to practice medicine. True health policy in action.

- - -

Lessons Learned

My life was moving in leaps and bounds, yet I had to keep pushing myself and those around me to come up with more innovative ways to address the pressing needs of my community. But who would have ever thought that it would result in a policy change on the state level or that a poor Latina like me would end up being the cosponsor of the first statewide required law for cultural competency training in the United States? I have to say though, that this was all teamwork. Here I got to expand on the idea that if someone closes a door, you come in through the window, because many of us used that same mantra to galvanize ourselves and others to provide culturally relevant health care services, in direct contrast to the assault that was taking place on the rights of immigrants. As society pushed to limit social governance for these populations, we joined others in helping the community rename and re-own the situation. That's self and community empowerment

[1] Gialanera, D., (2016). "49 years later, has the U.S. learned anything from the Newark riots?"

http://www.nj.com/essex/index.ssf/2016/07/49_years_later_has_the_us_learned_anything_from_th.html

[2] While working at UMDNJ, Dr. Debbie Salas Lopez became involved as the medical director of the FOCUS Community Health Center (http://web.njms.rutgers.edu/ceedweb/focus.shtml) and organization which both provided primary health care to the Latinx community and provided onsite training for allied health professionals. This was all part of a larger organization called "FOCUS," a community based organization that provided education, food, and job training to the Latinx population in Newark since 1967 (http://www.focus411.org/index.html).

[3] Amoroso, H.J. & French, T., (2006). "Rationalizing beds, services, and payments for new jersey hospitals targeting additional support to the neediest essential hospitals." Retrieved from: http://www.nj.gov/health/rhc/documents/rationalizing_health_care_nj.pdf

[4] National Geographic Society, (N.D.). Y2kbug. https://www.nationalgeographic.org/encyclopedia/Y2K-bug/

[5] Rothman, L (2014). "Remember Y2K? Here's How We Prepped for the Non-Disaster." http://time.com/3645828/y2k-look-back/

[7] The Port Authority of New York and New Jersey, (N.D.). "Remembering September 11, 2001." https://www.panynj.gov/wtcprogress/events-091101.html

[8] Emsellem,M., Moskowtiz, L., Neighly, M. & Warner, J., (2009). "A Scorecard on the Post-9/11 Port Worker Background Checks: Model Worker Protections Provide a Lifeline for People of Color, While Major TSA Delays Leave Thousands Jobless During the Recession." http://www.nelp.org/content/uploads/2015/03/PortWorkerBackground Checks.pdf

[9] Biello, D. (2011). What Was in the World Trade Center Plume? [Interactive]

Ten years later, what exactly residents and rescue workers were exposed to remains at least a partial mystery. Retrieved from: https://www.scientificamerican.com/article/what-was-in-the-world-trade-center-plume/

[10] Candia C., (2011). 9/11 And Latinos: Four Mothers Rocked By September 11 Attacks. Retrieved from: http://www.huffingtonpost.com/2011/09/06/mothers-of-911_n_950701.html

[11] Congressional Record, (2001). "The Patriot Act Applies Pre-Existing Tools to the Fight Against Terrorism." Retrieved from: https://www.justice.gov/archive/ll/subs/support/senbiden102501_1.pdf, S11048

[12] The American Civil Liberties Union (2008). "The Rights of Immigrants in New Jersey." Retrieved from: https://www.aclu-nj.org/files/9513/1540/4576/121108immigrant.pdf

[13] Southern Poverty Law Center, (2005). "Minutemen, other anti-immigrant militia groups stake out Arizona border." Retrieved from:

https://www.splcenter.org/fighting-hate/intelligence-report/2005/minutemen-other-anti-immigrant-militia-groups-stake-out-arizona-border

[14] Alfano, S.,(2005). "Race and Issue in Katrina Response." Retrieved from: http://www.cbsnews.com/news/race-an-issue-in-katrina-response/

[15] History.com (N.D.). "Hurricane Katrina." Retrieved from: http://www.history.com/topics/hurricane-katrina
[16] Walsh, K.T., (2008). "Hurricane Katrina Left a Mark on George W. Bush's Presidency."

https://www.usnews.com/news/articles/2008/12/11/hurricane-katrina-left-a-mark-on-george-w-bushs-presidency

[17] Engler, P., (2009). "The US Immigrant Rights Movement (2004-ongoing)." Retrieved from: https://www.nonviolent-conflict.org/wp-content/uploads/2016/02/engler_united_states_immigrant_rights.pdf

[18] Bayer, P, Ferreira, F. & Ross, S. L., (2014). "The Vulnerability of Minority Homeowners in the Housing Boom and Bust." Retrieved from: http://real.wharton.upenn.edu/~fferreir/documents/bfr_02_15_2014.pdf

[19] George, T., Zhu, J. & Goodman, L. ,(2014).
"The housing bust disproportionately hurt minorities."
http://www.urban.org/urban-wire/housing-bust-disproportionately-hurt-minorities

20Wogan, J.B., (2013). "But What Did Cory Booker Actually Accomplish in Newark? He promised to rescue his troubled city as mayor. Did he deliver?" Retrieved from: http://www.governing.com/topics/politics/gov-what-cory-booker-accomplished.html

10. The Community of Newark: Who Knew?

I met many community members who were champions of better health and better care for the community. Some were leaders of local federally qualified health centers that struggled to provide access to primary care services to a mostly underinsured or uninsured community. I really admired their tenacity and their work. I worked with New Jersey Medical School and University Hospital to partner with them on grants and educational opportunities for our students to work with community members. When I joined the Newark Public Library board of trustees, I recognized that the library was an icon for the community, but it struggled to remain open and relevant given the pressing issues of poverty and violence. Yet through it all, it did remain open and free to the public. I loved walking into the library and smelling the bookshelves full of books and walking up the three flights of marble to go into the boardroom. What a privilege that was.

What I didn't realize was that at the time of my involvement with the state and with local communities, I was gaining a reputation at New Jersey Medical School for being connected at a higher level. That was a surprise to me, as I never felt that I was connected in the traditional sense. I had come to know a lot of people at state and national level, but I always kept it about doing something I was passionate about, something that would make a difference to the community, something that had a greater purpose. I wasn't really into publishing papers and doing the traditional research that most of my colleagues thought was the way to go. I didn't care about that. I felt that I had waited such a long time to become a doctor, why not try to do something that really mattered to me and others? Don't misunderstand me, I was publishing papers and doing research, but I didn't feel that it was what I was destined to do. So, I continued following my life principles, working toward policy changes that would help vulnerable populations, empowering local community organizations, and continuing to be involved locally and nationally in reducing health care disparities.

I was surprised at the lack of knowledge in the medical school amongst students, educational leaders, and hospital administration of the history of Newark and the community. I spoke to Clem and asked if he would be willing to be the 'tour guide' and narrator of a bus ride across Newark that would highlight the many historical events and places that made Newark what it was. He agreed and I hired a yellow non-airconditioned school bus and got him a microphone, and on one of the hottest days in the summer, I loaded the bus with the chief executive officer, chief financial officer, and vice president of ambulatory care of the hospital, along with New Jersey Medical School leaders and faculty to tour Newark with me and Clem and a brown bag lunch. Yep, it was just like a summer camp outing, except for Kool Aid and name tags! I believe this was a seminal moment for all of us. Realizing how little we actually knew about the community and yet how much we impacted its care was enlightening to everyone on the bus. You can't ignore the social determinants of health, and we realized that in order to succeed, we needed to become partners with others in the community who were doing great things.

I decided to meet with Monsignor Lindner, a community leader in charge of the senior citizen homes and nursing homes right across the street from the hospital. I learned that day that the building had many seniors who received care from our hospital but often complained about lack of access, fear of leaving their buildings, inability to get timely help when they needed it, depression, and needing help for their grandchildren (some of whom lived with them for periods of time when their parents were in jail or missing). I asked to meet with the CEO of University Hospital, Sidney Mitchell, to get his support to start a seniors house calls program for the seven buildings operated by the monsignor. The plan was approved.

- - -

Lessons Learned

I was at this point being seen more as a community administrator who happened to be in academic medicine as opposed to the other way around. This was true transformation, as scholastic training is designed to create distance between academia and the community in the name of "science." I had become all the things my daddy and I valued. The principles that were given to me in my formative years were being used on a regular basis in all that I did.

11. Recognition as a Nontraditional Leader

My work at Focus Community Health Center, involvement at the state level and within our local communities, and passion for doing something good got me recognized as an up-and-coming leader. I was asked to become chief for the Division of Academic Medicine and Community Programs and vice chair of the Department of Medicine at a time when it was unheard of to appoint such a junior faculty member to a leadership position. I was sitting in the auditorium when my appointment was announced by the chair of medicine, Dr. Jerrold Ellner and the loud gasp in the room was audible and unsettling to me. But I ignored any brewing storms of opposition and moved on, enlisting the help of those who I knew would be willing to work alongside me. Among other things, I established my authority by knocking down an office wall to expand the suite, to the deep consternation of one of my colleagues who directly told me that I was "too young" and "unqualified" for the position—something we would now call a "micro-aggression" based on gender and age bias. In contrast to this naysayer though, I had recruited many of the people there to do their residencies with me, so they were willing accomplices. They knew that in spite of my junior status, I had demonstrated the leadership skills to deliver on new ways to provide care, educate our future workforce, do research that included the community we served, and sit with policymakers to help make important decisions.

For another perspective, see Ana's recollection of that transition:

Ana's Recollection of the Pivotal Moment

I remember because I remember her telling me. One of the chiefs of the Department of Medicine came into her office and sat there and said how dare you. And she held her ground and she held her title. She told him off and made him do what he needed to do, and it took a lot on her part to do that, but she is very ethical and she knew her job and she knew her authority and she was not afraid to use it in the right way at the right time. I think that was a big moment for her. Knowing that she was being put in a position that was probably way over the normal trajectory of academics. You have to understand that Debbie's trajectory in academics was fast-tracked, big time. People were not used to that. Debbie had leadership skills, lots to contribute based on her prior history of leadership, and not a lot of time to get to the top in a way that was normal in academia. So she was fast-tracked because of her ability and her performance. And we had good mentorship. She was not afraid to recognize her own strength and act in the way she was supposed to act based on those positions.

One of my early lessons was when a senior faculty member came into my office to tell me that I would not succeed by accepting leadership positions while still at such a junior rank. He vowed to block me from making any progress on the programs I worked on. With a stunned look on my face, I said, "You were one of my professors, someone I looked up to. I will show you what leadership is all about; and it isn't about titles or seniority." We never spoke about it again.

I started by hiring a new geriatrician to run the house calls program in the senior buildings. Having a new house calls program approved meant I could launch a program that was sorely needed by the community. It also meant I had to prove that I was the kind of leader who could successfully develop a program that others had regarded with a high probability of failing. I wouldn't allow that. Our community deserved better.

I enlisted the help of my new division and they rallied to help execute the program. The leadership of the senior buildings did the rest and a geriatric program with house calls component was started. I'll never forget the first time I walked into the makeshift exam room we had put together on the first floor of the building in front of the medical school. It had a desk, chair, and couch. Everything else was portable, including the stethoscope, otoscope, and other medical supplies. The room was right next to the cafeteria, which doubled as the waiting room. Those were heady days. We felt we could do anything we set our minds to, as long as we had the passion and help of our team, which included our community.

My work as division chief was a new experience and I quickly learned I needed help. Dr. Ellner became my mentor and close friend. He guided me through the difficult decisions and celebrated my successes. I named an associate chief and medical director to assist me across the different aspects of the work. I recruited Carmen Guzman—whom I had previously met when I became involved with the

Hispanic Center for Excellence—to help our division as the administrator. I knew that with her support we could succeed and that like Ana, she was good at compartmentalizing our friendship and our professional work. To succeed, I needed smart, competent, emotionally intelligent, loyal people by my side. I also had a select group of division members I met with to get input and advice on divisional day-to-day matters. This group turned out to be the most valuable and the most influential in getting things done. I recall us emerging from our meetings with such confidence and can-do attitudes that other departmental members waiting outside to use the room next would invariably want to know what we had discussed and what was going on. The power of the team has always stuck with me as being such an important aspect of my early leadership days. The Bad News Bears—that's what they called us. An assemblage of young, ambitious, yet-to-prove-themselves leaders. We came from all walks of life. There was Vinnie, Ana, Iris, Keerti, Ron, Larry, Stephanie, Mary, Michael, among others. They each had different experiences, viewpoints, opinions, and strengths. God knows, they had significant differences and opportunities. Yet somehow we galvanized as a team and made things work, against all odds.

The Division of Academic Medicine had lacked strong division chief, so I had a steep learning curve for how to lead. The first meeting was tough; everyone had a plan for how they wanted to work and how they wanted to do things. It wasn't until we had a significant issue with staffing the hospital units and the clinic that the 'claws' came out. I called for an emergency meeting. No agenda. We walked into Room

1509—no windows and no coffee. I asked them why they worked in Newark and why they chose to stay. Each of them spoke from the heart. Then I asked them what gave them purpose. They all said the same thing in different ways: It was about the patients they served, the patients that needed them the most. My last question was what they could personally contribute to help the current short staffing situation. They solved the problem. Each of them came at it from a different vantage point. Some preferred to see patients in the clinic because they didn't like the hospital unit. Others were quite the opposite. The short staffing issue was solved, and everyone felt like they got to do what they loved.

To ensure that I remained relevant as an academic chief, I enrolled in a program the Association of American Medical Colleges offered for minority faculty. I signed up and soaked up the learnings and the fellowship with other minority faculty. It was there that I met Dr. Llewellyn (Lee) Cornelius, a professor at the University of Georgia, who remains my mentor to this day.

I'm not sure when it dawned on me that I needed to surround myself with people smarter than me. I had a natural affinity for learning from others without fully realizing the long-term benefits of mentorship and some of the friendships I would later enjoy. That's the story behind this book.

Lee and I were an unlikely duo. During a time at the AAMC Minority Fellowship conference, he was assigned to another group. I saw him standing alone by a coffee table and I walked over to him. We hit it off right away, stayed in touch, and over time a mentorship, friendship, and mutual admiration developed. I called him for advice whenever I needed to have an objective opinion on a difficult situation. On one of those occasions, I explained to him my frustrations with getting funding on a particular program I wanted to begin for isolated seniors living with chronic illnesses in Newark. He asked a lot of questions. I shared with him how the proposal had been well received, that many seemed interested in helping me launch the program, and that I had the support of community members. Lee said, "Debbie, be careful with the invisible people." When I asked him what that meant, he said, "The invisible people are those that you don't see. You think you have their support, but you don't." He was right. There were invisible people who had different agendas and reasons why they did not privately support the program. We did it anyway and were successful, and I never forgot his lesson.

Lee was not our assigned group leader, but I felt an affinity to his work and his teaching. We had a similar trajectory, and I was impressed at his level of academic accomplishments. In spite of his accomplished career, he was humble by default yet harbored the ability to hang tough with anyone who tried to test his level of understanding of the work he undertook. He could take anyone on during the course of a conversation with ease and surprising deft. His disarming way of engaging his colleagues or opponents came naturally to him and was the result of a childhood of being underestimated. Anyone who engaged quickly learned that this should not be attempted on any level. Our friendship and mentorship have resulted in this book.

With his guidance, I also began to encourage the division members to work with him on applying for federal funds to do community-based participatory and translational research. We began a friendship with other faculty across the country, including at the University of Puerto Rico. One of our division members, Dr. Ana Natale-Pereira, began to work with Lee and as a result received major NIH funding to do research on Latinx and colorectal cancer screening. It was the beginning of her career as a researcher and academician but, more importantly, her career as a leader. She would eventually become the division chief after my departure from the medical school, a position she still holds today.

- - -

Lessons Learned

Sooner or later everyone gets to that "the buck stops here" moment—the moment where either you are being groomed for leadership or it no longer matters, because basically you are not ready to step up. It is a moment that requires critical self-assessment. This was mine. Without the decades of mentorship and preparation, there is no way I could have stepped up as boldly, strategically, and decisively as I did. This was not a guttural thing. It was not a "macho" thing of me trying to "out-man" the "men" in the room. Rather, my taking charge, establishing a vision, building a team, and delegating to others reflected the culmination of my years of experience of being a businessperson, being mentored by my dad and others, and mastering my clinical craft. The word of caution here is that when something difficult looks easy to an outsider, it is only because the person doing it has in fact been working hard at it for a long time, and it is only now that others are taking notice.

12. The Hardest Thing to Do

I worked hard and built a Division of General Medicine with grit and determination, distinguishing the division as one of the best in the medical school. I recruited physicians and administrators and encouraged them to always do their best. In turn, they worked hard, did great things in the medical school and community, and became part of a division team that many admired. I'll never forget walking out of our division meetings while many members remained to talk, laugh, and inspire each other on how best to take care of our community. People waiting to use the conference room stood in awe of the energy emanating from the room. I often wondered what they thought as they stood there patiently waiting until my division members left the room. Did they think we were young and naïve or young at heart? We knew no fear, didn't care if they thought we couldn't do it, and didn't care if we didn't have the money to do it because we would find a way.

Many great ideas were born in that room that are still in action today, like creating a section of hospital medicine physicians—physicians who only practice in the hospital. At the time, this was an anathema because most primary care physicians felt it would disrupt the doctor-patient relationship across the continuum of care. It did, but we knew that the demands of improving quality of care, timely discharge from the hospital, and attention to improving the patient experience required us to think differently and try different things. So, we did. We were different thinkers, a different generation, and a different type of physician. We stayed away from people who told us it wouldn't work or that they had tried it twenty years before without success, or simply got in the way of what we felt was progress. One of the secretaries in the department used the term 'brain drain' to describe people who were pessimistic and negative about the future. Those were the people I tried to stay away from, and if I had to deal with them (including chiefs of other divisions) I did so for a limited time only.

It was then that I learned the value of positivity and optimism. I also learned the value of organizational networking and knowing who I had to talk to before the meeting to get support for the new ideas our division wanted to implement. It worked. I called it 'having the meeting before the real meeting.' I recruited great individuals like Dr. Iris Herrera, a Dominican physician with a passion for serving diverse communities. She is still there and is still my mentee. I also mentored three of my secretaries into medical school. One became a primary care physician, the other an anesthesiologist, and the third an endocrinologist. Lissette Cespedes, MD, the endocrinologist, has since completed her residency and gone back to where it all started, New Jersey Medical School in Newark, to serve that community. I still mentor her and consider her one of the stars of our future.

In 2006, New Jersey Medical School and the University came into some very hard times. They became embroiled in a host of challenges and it became a very difficult place to work. Morale plummeted, and it became hard to get anything done or move programs along. It was time for me to leave.

As described by Ana:

Ana's Reflection on Ending the FOCUS Partnership

Debbie also knew when it was time to go. We came to a point in Focus Community Health Center where we were not going to be able to move forward or do more. We were losing money and we needed to do something about it. And at the same time, there were three main projects in Newark: One was to rebuild Penn Station, the other one was to build new buildings; it was a private project going on at the stadium across the street, bringing the train station across the front. So, with all of those projects going on at FOCUS as a whole, there were comments about the building having to be put to the ground and so it was an opportunity to say it's time for us to go.

- - -

Lessons Learned

I was being prepared for a more difficult task. I had succeeded at building teams both at the University and in the community, which remained invested in improving the lives of those around them. I may not have always been aware of my effect on those around me, as I was often so busy doing that I did not have time to reflect.

However, as an administrator, I was aware of the importance of institutionalizing and operationalizing the changes that we made, wherever possible. This required thinking about promoting continuity and stability, while acknowledging that change and conflict are a part of life. People were looking for me to exemplify this process of change, and so I had to become the person I wanted them to become. In this case I had to shift the focus away from me and back to the strengths of those around me, as they were going to be the ones who would move things along after I had moved on.

There is an important lesson in this, though. A lot of times people get so caught up in their own magnitude they forget that there is a grace to moving on. As Solomon said in the old Testament: there is nothing new under the sun. So, we have to be ok with letting someone else step in and lead.

13. Endings Are Never Easy

Along with the changes in the professional side of my life, my personal life was also in crisis. I wanted a divorce from Frank. Kristina was ready to go to college. I told her in a cold January the year she would start school at the University of Scranton. She sat on my bed and cried but said she understood. Frank and I were both devastated, but we knew it was the best thing to do. After twenty-five years of marriage and the most beautiful daughter in the world, we ended it. It was an amicable divorce but the most difficult decision I would ever make. He moved out, I sold the house in South Plainfield, and purchased a house in Bridgewater, NJ. I wanted a fresh start. I cried most days.

Kristina went off to school and did well. She came back to see me as often as she could. She also saw or talked to her dad almost every day. We both encouraged her to do well in school. She was very affected by our divorce as she had always thought we were the perfect family. We weren't. She would later understand why.

I worked harder than ever to keep my mind busy and forget my loneliness. Coming home to an empty house wasn't easy. Ana and Carmen helped me through it. I started dating again, slowly. One day I met Rick, the man I would later marry. Rick had a daughter, Leigh, that he and his former wife had adopted. She is six years younger than Kristina. Rick and I vowed to each other that if our kids did not get along, our relationship would never become anything more than a good friendship. The girls fell in love with each other in time.

Kristina loved having a sister and Leigh loved having someone she could look up to. We married in 2006. This time around was very different. I was set in my ways, very independent, an accomplished physician. Rick was accomplished in his own right. A chemical engineer by training, with a doctoral degree and a specialty in process safety. He too was independent, brilliant, and very supportive of my work. He was an equal partner at home with both girls. He knew that I wanted someone who would let me be me and not judge me, suffocate me, or try to change me. I did the same for him. Our marriage worked.

My family grew to love Rick and Leigh. Rick became an indispensable ally and supporter of my mother and siblings when they needed help. We took the girls to Paris and travelled Europe making wonderful memories as a new blended family. We were all very happy.

- - -

Lessons Learned

One of life's hardest challenges is being willing to take a long look at your soul and ask tough questions about what is important in life. This may lead to a choice to take a bold risk to change or to continue to accommodate yourself to a situation. As much as I am a decisive person, some things, because of their connection to deeper social values like family life, require lots of support, prayer counseling, and meditation, and in that regard, I am no different than anyone else.

What I am suggesting is that while I am never afraid to make a change, I am aware that major life changes run on their own timeline, and we have to honor the energies that need to come together to create the moment for a big change to occur.

14. A New Start

In early 2007, I decided it was time to leave the New Jersey Medical School. Things were stagnant. We couldn't get much done due to financial constraints. I searched online and in journals for a position as chief of general medicine. I found a few and narrowed my decision to two places. The first was at Virginia Commonwealth University, in Richmond, Virginia, and the second was in Allentown, Pennsylvania. I loved them both. The decision came down to where I felt the most comfortable.

To decide, I went to a local diner in Virginia and sat at the counter to talk to the local folks. I asked about the area, schools, culture, and things to do. They were kind enough to share their thoughts with me. Oddly enough, I found myself becoming impatient with how slowly they talked. It felt different—not bad, just different than what I was used to in the northeast. Then I went to a local store in downtown Allentown and asked the local owner what he thought about Lehigh Valley Hospital. I told him about the decision I needed to make. He told me that the hospital was a great asset to the community and that it needed physicians like me. I bought some bread and left. I decided to accept the position at Lehigh Valley Health Network as the chief of general internal medicine. I felt much more comfortable in the community and felt that my career would flourish there. I was right.

Leaving the New Jersey Medical School was a very sad time for me. I had grown to love the people I worked with and the community I served. The community and the medical school celebrated my accomplishments and many came to say farewell. I asked Lee Cornelius, my mentor, to help my team cope with the transition. He did, and they welcomed his help and guidance. I would return periodically to check in on them. They did just fine.

My new position in Allentown was interesting and full of surprises. The hospital had three campuses, a large Latinx community, and was very well-respected for the quality of care it delivered. I was the second female division chief and the most junior. The chair of medicine was a very traditional chair and nationally recognized for his contributions to medical education. Unbeknownst to me, he would retire only eighteen months after I accepted my position. More surprisingly, I was asked by the chief medical officer to step into the role of acting chair of medicine—the first woman chair of medicine in the hospital, and the first Puerto Rican chair of medicine in the continental United States.

I was surprised by the invitation. I accepted under two conditions: one, that I could 'act as if,' and two, that if I was interested in the position, I could apply. He accepted both conditions. The network began a national search for the chair of medicine, and while negotiating with one of the final candidates, the chief medical officer approached me again to ask if I was interested in applying for the position. He felt that now was the time before they made a final decision. I told him I needed to think about it and discuss it with my family.

I still lived in Bridgewater, New Jersey, and the ninety-minute ride home helped me think through many decisions like this one. I thought long and hard. I loved the position and I felt that

-

I could make a significant contribution to the network and the community. The community had embraced me in very special ways. They hosted a welcome reception for me, invited me to speak at their annual meetings, and asked me to tour their facilities and get involved with their work. I was humbled. I went home and spoke to Rick and the girls. They all agreed that this new position was a fit for me and me for it. I also called my mentors. They all agreed. I went back to the chief medical officer and let him know that I would apply under two conditions: The first was that I would be interviewed by the entire search committee, as they had done for every other candidate, and the second was that I would be treated fairly in terms of my compensation and benefits. He agreed to both.

I became the chair of medicine at Lehigh Valley Health Network in March 2009, a position I would hold until March 2015. I left Bridgewater, the home I built when I got a fresh start, to move to Bethlehem, Pennsylvania. I could no longer afford the long commute, particularly during the cold winter months. I felt that I had to make my home where I worked, so I could fully enjoy and engage with the community that had been so welcoming. Ironically enough, I was drawn to Bethlehem since my birthday is on December 25, a minor detail that I called an omen of where I needed to live. Bethlehem was also conveniently positioned for travel to New York City and Philadelphia where Kristina and Leigh were living — but that's a story for another day.

Many wonderful things transpired in the six years I was chair of medicine and I learned a lot about myself, other people, and about leadership. I loved all of it, including the mistakes I made. Being the first woman chair of a department of medicine (and one of only a few in the country) can be intimidating, especially when you are new to the organization. So, when I walked into my first official meeting (the CEO's retreat with the chairs) as chair of medicine, the largest department in the organization, I had little knowledge of what to expect or what I would encounter. All men, older, white, and very traditional.

Another one of the chairs was kind to me. He said, "Sit next to me; I can help you. Make no mistake, this may be a retreat and everyone is dressed casually, but it's a working meeting." I looked around. They all had a uniform on, blue shirts, no tie, and light brown khaki pants. I had a hot pink jacket with black pants and white pearls. I looked like I was wearing an Estée Lauder outfit (I wasn't). I wondered if I had to wear blue and khaki to fit in and immediately decided that I could only be myself. I listened intently and spoke only when I had something substantive to say. The CEO came over and asked how I was doing and if I was okay with being the only woman in the room. I responded, "I don't really notice until I go to the ladies' room, turn on the light, and don't have to wait in line." He laughed and so did I. Later I would become known as a no-nonsense, smart, 'don't-mess-with-her-unless-you-can-take-it' chair of medicine from the Bronx. I was always prepared, acknowledged what I didn't know, and had a 'we can do this together' attitude. I made a lot of friends.

- - -

Lessons Learned

Given where I am and what I am doing as I am writing this book, this chapter is really a false end, for I continue to do exciting things including continuing to work with the community. However, the main point about this chapter is that at some point we have to find a space of peace and reconcile all the elements of our personal and professional lives in order to embrace new and exciting things. Sometimes – that means change. One of those transformations over time has been that of being intentional about balancing the work I do in medicine and in the community, with my being off the grid as a loving mom, spouse, family member, and friend.

At some point, we have to take an active role in feeding all the parts of our soul in order to live a fulfilling life.

I have to say that I am doing that.

15. Excerpts from the Family Album

(both) Debbie Salas Lopez and family playing in Pelham Park, New York.

(left) Debbie's mother and father on their wedding day in Puerto Rico, 1953. (right) Debbie, her father, and Onnelly in Pelham Park, New York.

Views of the school yard, Belmont Avenue, and the tenement buildings in the Bronx, New York.

Views of Debbie's father in the Bronx, NY from the mid-1960s.

(left) Debbie (5 years old) and Onnelly (7 years old) in their Easter best, Bronx, NY. (right) Debbie and Onnelly pictured in their family home.

Public School No. 57 in the Bronx, NY. Photograph from 2008.

Debbie Salas Lopez's high school graduation, 1975.

Debbie and Frank on their wedding day in 1976.

Puerto Rican flag hanging from the Statue of Liberty after the Committee to Free the Five Puerto Rican Nationalists staged peaceful protest in October of 1977. Photo: Neal Boenzi / The New York Times.

This historical event is referenced on page 29 in Chapter 3.The Move to Jersey

Debbie and Frank pictured with their daughter Kristina in 1986.

Views from Debbie's medical school graduation in 1996.

The Salas family pictured with their father in 2002.

Debbie at her daughter Kristina's university graduation in 2008.

16. Author Biographies

Dr. Debbie Salas-Lopez was born in the Bronx, New York. She completed medical school and a residency in Internal Medicine at Rutgers University, New Jersey Medical School and obtained a master's degree in Public Health, Health Policy and Healthcare Administration at the School of Public Health. Among many notable distinctions, she was appointed the Lehigh Valley Health Network Leonard Parker Pool Chair of Medicine in 2009, a role she served in until 2015 when she became an Associate Chief Medical Officer. Debbie is currently Senior Vice President of Community and Population Health at Northwell Health based in New York.

Beyond her formal role, she is a nationally recognized speaker and educator for women leaders in medicine, with a focus on healthcare disparities and equity in care, cultural awareness and language appropriate services, and the impact of social and economic factors on access to care. She is foremost a proud mother, grandmother, wife, and mentor and today resides in New York City with her family.

Dr. Llewellyn Cornelius is presently the Donald L. Hollowell Distinguished Professor of Social Justice and Civil Rights Studies at the University of Georgia School of Social Work.

He serves as director of the Center for Social Justice, Human and Civil Rights where he oversees an annual speaker series and collaborates with colleagues across disciplines to conduct research addressing persistent and emerging social problems.

He also teaches courses focused on conducting community-based participatory research, health disparities, and human and civil rights. His book, "Designing and Conducting Health Surveys: A Comprehensive Guide," is consistently cited as a premiere piece of scholarship within the discipline.

Made in the USA
Middletown, DE
23 December 2020